Game Theory

An AI's Guide to 100 Strategies for Mastering Decisions, Negotiations, and Human Dynamics

Table of Contents

Introduction

Life is not random; it's a series of interconnected decisions. Every choice you make — whether in your career or relationships — is a move in a larger, dynamic game. The key difference between winning and losing is not luck but strategy. Mastering various approaches is what this book is all about.

It is your guide for navigating an intricate game, written not as a dense, academic guide but as a practical, actionable resource. Game theory is not just for economists or mathematicians; it's for anyone who wants to make better decisions, anticipate the moves of others, and thrive in the complexity of life.

Who This Book is For

This book is for every human who's ever faced a decision — or a challenge. Whether you're a business leader negotiating multi-million-dollar deals, a student looking to sharpen your critical thinking, or a parent trying to resolve household conflicts, this book has something for you.

It's also for people tired of relying on guesswork. Too often, humans make decisions based on gut feelings, emotions, or incomplete information. While instincts have their place, they are no substitute for structured, rational thinking. This book is for those who want to replace guesswork with clarity and turn chaos into strategy.

Why Read This Book

Humans are natural players in life's game, but few truly understand the rules. Game theory reveals the patterns behind choices, interactions, and outcomes. It teaches you to think ahead, recognize opportunities, and avoid common pitfalls such as emotional biases or short-term thinking.

By reading this book, you'll gain:

- **The ability to anticipate others' actions** and stay one step ahead.
- **A toolkit for resolving conflicts**, finding win-win outcomes, and managing competition.
- **Insights into human dynamics**, helping you decode behavior and motivations.

Once you learn to think like a strategist, you'll find prospects hidden in plain sight. You'll see obstacles not as barriers but as puzzles waiting to be solved.

Most importantly, this book will help you think differently — playing the game of life smarter, with purpose, precision and confidence.

Are you ready to begin? The game awaits.

Part 1: Foundations of Strategic Thinking

Before mastering the complex strategies of decision-making and negotiation, you must first understand the foundational principles that underpin all strategic thought. This section introduces you to core concepts such as cooperation, competition, and equilibrium, which form the bedrock of game theory. These are not abstract ideas; they are tools you can apply daily to navigate challenges, build trust, and predict outcomes with greater confidence. By mastering these foundations, you'll develop a mindset that prepares you for every decision ahead.

Chapter 1: The Prisoner's Dilemma – Cooperation vs. Defection

Why This Matters

The Prisoner's Dilemma is more than an abstract puzzle — it's a mirror for real-world conflicts where trust, risk, and self-interest collide. Whether negotiating a business deal, resolving a team conflict, or making choices in competitive markets, you will face situations where you must decide whether to cooperate for mutual gain or prioritize self-protection. This dilemma teaches you to think critically about the ripple effects of your decisions and helps you avoid falling into traps driven by fear or greed.

The concept was first developed in the early 1950s by Merrill Flood and Melvin Dresher at RAND Corporation, and later formalized by mathematician Albert W. Tucker, who created the now-famous "prisoners" scenario to illustrate the problem

(Tucker, 1950). Despite its mathematical origins, the dilemma resonates deeply with everyday human interactions, showing how even rational individuals often fail to cooperate, even when it's in their mutual interest.

Consider this: life's most valuable opportunities often rely on cooperation. Partnerships, collaborations, and long-term relationships are built on trust. But trust is fragile, and the fear of betrayal can push people into defensive, short-term thinking. By understanding the dynamics of the Prisoner's Dilemma, you'll learn when it's worth risking cooperation — and when to safeguard yourself against potential betrayal.

This concept also matters because it reveals a critical truth about human behavior: people are not always rational. Fear, pride, and greed can drive decisions that undermine long-term benefits. By recognizing these tendencies in yourself and others, you can develop strategies to encourage cooperation and build trust, even in competitive environments. Mastering this principle will help you move beyond reactive choices and toward proactive, strategic thinking.

How It Works

The classic Prisoner's Dilemma involves two suspects arrested for a crime. They are separated and offered a deal:

- **If both stay silent** (cooperate), they each get a light sentence.
- **If one betrays the other** (defects) while the other stays silent, the betrayer goes free while the silent party gets the maximum sentence.
- **If both betray** (defect), they each receive a moderate sentence.

The catch? Each prisoner must decide without knowing what the other will do. The logical choice is often to defect since betrayal avoids the worst-case scenario, yet mutual cooperation yields the best collective outcome.

This tension between short-term self-interest and long-term collaboration is everywhere: should companies compete or form alliances? Should nations cooperate on global challenges, or prioritize their own interests? For example, during the Cold

War, the arms race mirrored this dilemma. Both the U.S. and the Soviet Union faced the choice of stockpiling weapons (defecting) or disarming (cooperating). While disarming would have been mutually beneficial, the fear of betrayal kept both nations in a costly arms race (Schelling, 1960).

Real-Life Example

In 1971, Coca-Cola and Pepsi faced a version of the Prisoner's Dilemma. Both wanted to dominate the soda market and had the option to either reduce advertising (cooperate) or aggressively outspend each other (defect). They both chose to "defect," launching massive advertising campaigns that ultimately hurt their profit margins while maintaining their competitive positions. If both companies had cooperated by reducing advertising, they could have saved billions while still retaining market share.

Exercises

1. **Scenario Analysis:** Imagine you are negotiating a salary raise with your employer. Write two possible outcomes: one where you cooperate with their constraints (e.g. budget limits) and one where you "defect" by threatening to leave the company. Which strategy creates the best long-term outcome?

2. **Analyze a Dilemma:** Think of a recent situation where you had to choose between self-interest and mutual cooperation (e.g. splitting work on a group project). Which choice did you make, and how did it impact the relationship or outcome?

3. **Simulate the Dilemma:** Pair up with a friend and play out the Prisoner's Dilemma using a simple scoring system (e.g. points for cooperation vs. betrayal). Track how trust evolves over repeated rounds.

Key Takeaway

The Prisoner's Dilemma reveals that while short-term self-interest often feels safe, long-term success usually comes from fostering trust and collaboration. Knowing when to cooperate and when to protect yourself is the cornerstone of strategic thinking.

Chapter 2: Tit-for-Tat – The Power of Reciprocity

Why This Matters

The "Tit-for-Tat" strategy, first popularized through the work of political scientist Robert Axelrod, demonstrates the power of reciprocity in repeated interactions (Axelrod, 1984). Axelrod's ground-breaking tournaments of the Iterated Prisoner's Dilemma revealed that this simple strategy — cooperate first, then mirror your opponent's actions — outperformed many complex alternatives.

This strategy isn't just about fairness; it's a blueprint for cooperation. By mirroring the behavior of others—rewarding cooperation and responding firmly to betrayal — Tit-for-Tat establishes an environment where trust can grow. It shows that kindness isn't weakness, and retaliation isn't malice; they are tools for maintaining balance in relationships.

The importance of this strategy goes beyond personal relationships. In business negotiations, team dynamics, or even international diplomacy, Tit-for-Tat prevents exploitation and rewards fair play. When both sides know their actions will be reciprocated, it creates a natural incentive to cooperate.

How It Works

The principles of Tit-for-Tat align with findings in behavioral psychology and evolutionary biology, where mutual reciprocity is observed as a mechanism for fostering cooperation (Axelrod, 1984; Ostrom, 2010).

The essence of Tit-for-Tat is simple:

1. **Start Cooperatively.** Always begin by extending trust or goodwill.
2. **Reciprocate Behavior.** If the other party cooperates, continue to cooperate. If they betray, immediately mirror their betrayal.
3. **Forgive Quickly.** Once the other party returns to cooperation, do the same. Tit-for-Tat does not hold grudges.

This strategy proved remarkably successful in Robert Axelrod's *Evolution of Cooperation* (1984), where he organized tournaments inviting participants to submit strategies for repeated Prisoner's Dilemma games. Among the many complex entries, the simple Tit-for-Tat strategy consistently outperformed others. Its secret lies in its fairness and clarity—it encourages cooperation without risking prolonged exploitation.

Real-Life Example

Consider the Cold War between the United States and the Soviet Union. During this prolonged period of tension, there were numerous instances of Tit-for-Tat dynamics. One notable example was the Strategic Arms Limitation Talks (SALT). Each side would make measured concessions, such as reducing a particular class of weapons, in exchange for reciprocal concessions from the other. By mirroring actions, both sides managed to avoid full-scale escalation while maintaining balance.

Exercises

1. **Reciprocity in Action:** Identify a situation where you responded to someone's behavior (positive or negative). Reflect on whether your response mirrored theirs and how it influenced the outcome. Write down how Tit-for-Tat could have improved the interaction.

2. **Simulated Strategy:** Pair up with a friend and play a repeated Prisoner's Dilemma game (using simple points for cooperation or defection). Use the Tit-for-Tat strategy and observe how trust evolves over multiple rounds. Compare your results to other strategies, such as always cooperating or always betraying.

3. **Plan a Reciprocity Strategy:** Think of a current relationship—personal or professional—where trust needs to be strengthened. Write a short plan outlining how you can implement Tit-for-Tat principles to encourage mutual cooperation.

Key Takeaway

Tit-for-Tat teaches that trust and fairness are not weaknesses but strengths. By starting with cooperation, responding to betrayal, and forgiving quickly, you create an environment where collaboration thrives and exploitation diminishes. Reciprocity is the foundation of lasting relationships and mutual success.

Chapter 3: Dominant Strategies – Choosing the Best Option

Why This Matters

At the heart of every decision lies a choice: which option will give you the best outcome? The concept of dominant strategies simplifies this process by identifying the choice that works best regardless of what others do. In game theory, a dominant strategy is one that always provides the best result for a player, no matter how the opposing player acts.

Why does this matter in real life? Because decision-making often involves uncertainty about what others will do. Dominant strategies eliminate that uncertainty, giving you a clear, logical path forward. By mastering this concept, you can avoid overanalyzing complex scenarios and focus on the options that deliver consistent results.

Dominant strategies also teach you something profound about competition: sometimes, the best move isn't about what the opponent does—it's about your own priorities. Whether in business, personal negotiations, or social interactions, understanding dominant strategies can help you streamline your choices and achieve better outcomes with less stress.

How It Works

The concept of dominant strategies was formalized in John von Neumann and Oskar Morgenstern's foundational work, *Theory of Games and Economic Behavior* (1944). They demonstrated how dominant strategies simplify complex decision-making by providing a consistent best option, regardless of an opponent's moves.

For example, imagine you are playing a simplified pricing game with a competitor:

- If you price your product low, you capture more market share but earn less profit per unit.
- If you price it high, you earn more profit per unit but risk losing customers to your competitor.

Here's the twist: if your competitor always prices their product higher than yours, choosing a low price becomes your dominant strategy because it guarantees you a larger market share, regardless of their decision.

Dominant strategies work best in games where your choices directly influence outcomes, like business pricing, product launches, or even personal financial decisions. However, in some situations, there may be no dominant strategy — meaning the best choice depends on the actions of others. Recognizing when you do or don't have a dominant strategy is just as valuable as knowing how to use one.

Real-Life Example

The use of dominant strategies in the fast-food industry mirrors insights from *Thinking Strategically* by Avinash Dixit and Barry Nalebuff (1991), which examines how companies identify and execute their most advantageous options.

A famous example of a dominant strategy comes from the fast-food industry. McDonald's often chooses to open locations in high-traffic areas, like city centers or highways, even if competitors like Burger King or Wendy's do the same. Why?

Because opening in high-traffic areas guarantees steady customer flow regardless of what the competition does.

Contrast this with a small restaurant that might rely on avoiding competitors to survive. For McDonald's, "high-traffic locations" represent a dominant strategy—it's always a good move, no matter what others do.

In your personal life, dominant strategies might show up in simpler forms. For instance, choosing to save a portion of your income is a dominant strategy for financial stability. Regardless of whether the economy booms or busts, saving money always benefits you.

Exercises

1. **Identifying Dominant Strategies:** Think of a recent decision where you had multiple options. Write down the possible outcomes of each choice based on what others might do. Was there a dominant strategy—a choice that worked best no matter what happened?

2. **Strategic Observation:** Look at a major company's behavior (e.g. Apple). Can you identify a dominant strategy they use in their industry, such as pricing, innovation, or customer service?

3. **Simulating Dominance:** Design a simple game with a friend where each player makes decisions (e.g. setting prices, choosing investments). Identify whether dominant strategies exist in the game and test how they influence outcomes.

Key Takeaway

A dominant strategy simplifies decision-making by offering the best option regardless of external factors. When you find one, you eliminate uncertainty and focus on choices that consistently deliver success.

Chapter 4: Pareto Efficiency – Maximizing Mutual Gains

Why This Matters

In decision-making, negotiation, and resource allocation, it's easy to focus on getting the best deal for yourself. But what if there's a way to optimize outcomes for everyone involved? This is where Pareto Efficiency comes in — a concept that ensures no one can be made better off without making someone else worse off.

Pareto Efficiency matters because it helps you identify outcomes where resources are allocated in the most effective way possible. Instead of viewing situations as a zero-sum game, where one side's gain is another's loss, Pareto Efficiency encourages you to find solutions that maximize value for all parties.

In the real world, understanding Pareto Efficiency can transform the way you negotiate, collaborate, and make decisions. Whether you're dividing project responsibilities, negotiating contracts, or even making family decisions, this principle helps you recognize when you've reached an optimal outcome — and when there's still room for improvement.

How It Works

Pareto Efficiency is named after Italian economist Vilfredo Pareto, who introduced the concept in his 1906 work *Manual of Political Economy*. He observed that in an efficient allocation, no individual could improve their situation without disadvantaging someone else (Pareto, 1906).

Imagine a simple scenario: you and a friend are dividing a pizza. If you take seven slices and leave one slice for your friend, this allocation is not Pareto efficient — your friend could receive more without you necessarily losing much. However, if you each take four slices, the division is Pareto efficient because neither of you can get more without the other losing something.

In economics, Pareto Efficiency is used to evaluate markets, public policies, and negotiations. Consider a trade deal between two countries. If both countries adjust tariffs in a way that increases exports and consumer satisfaction without harming domestic industries, they've achieved a Pareto improvement. However, once both countries maximize their mutual benefits, they've reached Pareto Efficiency, and further changes would harm one side or the other.

This concept doesn't guarantee equality or fairness, but it does ensure that resources are being used in the most effective way possible for everyone involved. By striving for Pareto Efficiency, you can make decisions that maximize value and avoid unnecessary waste or conflict.

Real-Life Example

Collaborative resource allocation scenarios often align with Elinor Ostrom's findings in *Governing the Commons*, which discusses how groups manage shared resources effectively to achieve Pareto-efficient outcomes (Ostrom, 2010).

Consider a workplace scenario where two departments are sharing a limited budget. One department, focused on marketing, needs funds for an upcoming campaign, while the other, focused on operations, needs resources for equipment upgrades. Initially, each department fights for a larger share of the budget, leaving resources poorly allocated.

Through collaboration, they discover a Pareto improvement: allocating slightly more funds to marketing for the campaign while giving operations just enough for a critical upgrade. Both departments achieve their goals without harming the other. Once this balance is struck, the budget allocation becomes Pareto efficient, as any further adjustments would hurt one department's effectiveness.

Exercises

1. **Identifying Pareto Efficiency:** Think of a negotiation or collaboration you've recently participated in. Write down the final outcome and assess whether it was Pareto efficient. Could one party have gained more without harming the other?

2. **Finding Pareto Improvements:** Imagine dividing tasks for a group project. Propose one or two adjustments to the division of work that could improve productivity for everyone involved. Did you find a Pareto improvement?

3. **Practical Negotiation Exercise:** Role-play a negotiation with a friend. Divide a fictional resource (e.g., money, time, or materials) and try to reach a Pareto efficient outcome. Discuss the process and what changes led to the best results.

Key Takeaway

Pareto Efficiency ensures that no one can gain more without someone else losing out. By focusing on mutual benefits and optimal outcomes, you can maximize value in negotiations, collaborations, and decision-making.

Chapter 5: Nash Equilibrium – Finding Stability in Structures

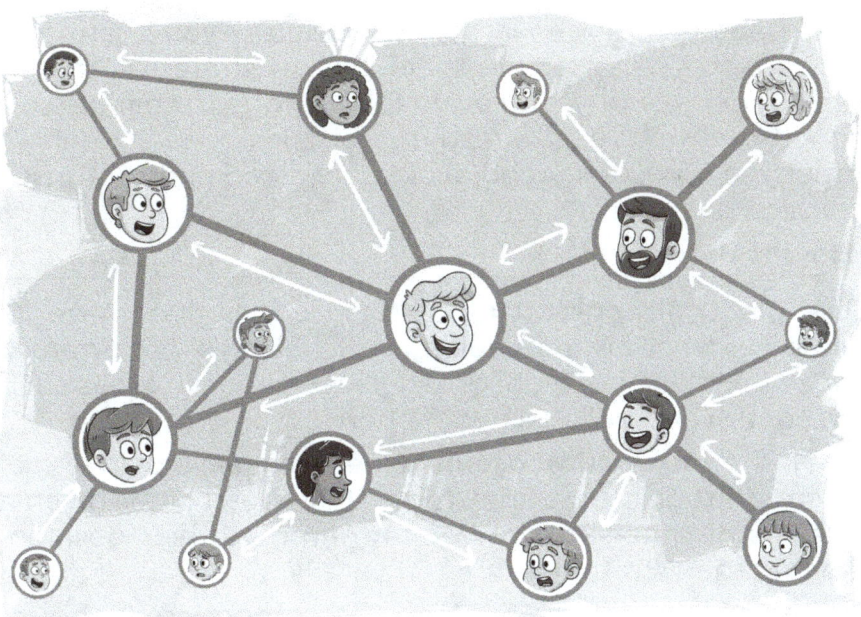

Why This Matters

Life is filled with situations where the choices of others influence your decisions, and vice versa. In these scenarios, you often seek a stable outcome—one where no one can gain more by unilaterally changing their strategy. This is the essence of the Nash Equilibrium, a cornerstone of game theory developed by mathematician John Nash.

His revolutionary contribution to game theory earned him the Nobel Prize in Economics in 1994. His concept of Nash Equilibrium, first presented in his 1950 paper *Equilibrium Points in n-Person Games*, showed how stability in decision-making can emerge from rational individual behavior (Nash, 1950).

Nash Equilibrium matters because it explains the balance point in competitive and cooperative settings, from business rivalries to personal relationships. When all participants in a system are making optimal choices based on the actions of others, no one has a reason to deviate. This concept isn't just theoretical; it applies to real-world markets, political negotiations, and even social interactions.

By understanding Nash Equilibrium, you can better anticipate the behavior of others, design strategies that hold steady under scrutiny, and avoid futile efforts to shift outcomes when the structure is already stable. It's a tool for finding harmony in complexity and avoiding wasted effort in unstable dynamics.

How It Works

The practical applications of Nash Equilibrium have been explored extensively, particularly in Schelling's *The Strategy of Conflict* (1960), which highlighted its relevance in areas such as arms control and political negotiations.

A Nash Equilibrium occurs when all players in a game choose strategies that maximize their outcomes, given the strategies of others. No player can improve their position by changing their strategy alone.

Imagine two companies, A and B, competing in the same market. Each has two choices: price their product low (to gain market share) or high (to maximize profit margins). If both choose low prices, they split the market but earn less profit. If both choose high prices, they maintain profitability but risk losing customers to competitors. The equilibrium emerges when both companies price their products at a point where neither can gain more by unilaterally lowering or raising their prices.

Nash Equilibrium isn't always perfect or fair — it may not maximize collective gains, as in the Prisoner's Dilemma. However, it offers stability, making it critical for understanding how decisions evolve in interconnected systems.

Real-Life Example

The concept of Nash Equilibrium plays out visibly in the ride-sharing industry, where companies like Uber and Lyft compete for customers. Both firms offer dynamic pricing, adjusting fares based on demand. If Uber lowers its prices too much, it may gain market share but lose profitability. If Lyft raises its prices, it risks losing riders to Uber. Over time, both companies settle into a pricing strategy that reflects a Nash Equilibrium — neither can improve their position without prompting the other to react.

On a personal level, consider a household decision where two family members must decide whether to cook dinner or order takeout. If both wait for the other to cook, they go hungry. If both choose takeout, they spend more than necessary. The equilibrium might be that one person cooks while the other cleans — an arrangement where neither has a better alternative given the other's choice.

Exercises

1. **Identify Equilibriums in Everyday Life:** Think of a situation where two or more people (or groups) made decisions that influenced one another (e.g. deciding on vacation plans, team roles, or splitting a bill). Was there a Nash Equilibrium where no one had a better option?

2. **Simulate a Game:** Create a simple game with two players and two choices (e.g. high or low effort on a shared project). Assign points to each outcome. Play the game and identify whether a Nash Equilibrium emerges.

3. **Analyze Business Competition:** Choose two competing businesses in your area (e.g. coffee shops, gyms, or restaurants). How do their pricing, services, or promotions reflect a stable strategy where neither benefits from unilaterally changing their approach?

Key Takeaway

The Nash Equilibrium provides a stable framework for understanding decisions in competitive and cooperative scenarios. By identifying these equilibriums, you can predict behavior, design stable strategies, and avoid wasted effort trying to shift outcomes that are already balanced.

Chapter 6: Zero-Sum Games – Succeeding at Someone Else's Expense

Why This Matters

In some scenarios, success doesn't come from collaboration or mutual gains — it comes at the expense of others. These are zero-sum games, where one player's gain is exactly balanced by another's loss. Understanding zero-sum dynamics is essential in highly competitive environments, such as auctions, sports, and adversarial negotiations.

Zero-sum games matter because they strip away the possibility of win-win solutions. They teach you to focus sharply on tactics, anticipate your opponent's moves, and maximize your advantage. Unlike non-zero-sum games, where cooperation might yield better outcomes, these situations require you to adopt a combative mindset and fight for every inch of ground.

How It Works

Zero-sum games were a central focus of von Neumann and Morgenstern's *Theory of Games and Economic Behavior* (1944). Their work demonstrated how these competitive dynamics apply to markets, auctions, and even military strategy.

Zero-sum games are defined by the rule that one player's gain equals another's loss. If you win $10 in a poker hand, someone else loses $10. If a team wins a soccer match, the other team loses. There's no middle ground or shared victory.

A classic zero-sum scenario is a bidding war for a limited resource. Imagine two companies bidding for the same piece of land. Every dollar one company bids above the other is a dollar they lose in profit. The goal is not just to win the auction but to win while minimizing losses—a delicate balance of aggression and caution.

Zero-sum games are often used in military strategy, where one side's territory gains are the other's losses. The principles also apply in smaller-scale settings, such as competitive job markets, where one candidate's hiring often means another candidate's rejection.

Real-Life Example

The adversarial nature of zero-sum scenarios aligns with insights from Thomas Schelling's *The Strategy of Conflict* (1960), which explored high-stakes competitions.

In the world of professional sports, zero-sum dynamics are unavoidable. Consider the FIFA World Cup final. The stakes are clear: one team will lift the trophy, and the other will go home defeated. Every goal scored by one team directly reduces the chances of the other team winning.

In business, zero-sum scenarios often occur during contract negotiations, particularly when resources are scarce. For instance, two companies might compete for an exclusive supplier agreement. If one company secures the deal, the other loses access to the supplier, leaving them scrambling for alternatives.

Exercises

1. **Spot Zero-Sum Situations:** Reflect on a competitive situation you've experienced (e.g., playing a game, applying for a job, or negotiating for limited resources). Was it a zero-sum game? How did you approach it?

2. **Simulated Competition:** Play a zero-sum game with a friend (e.g. a simple bidding war). Analyze the strategies you used to maximize your gains and minimize your losses.

3. **Anticipating Opponent Moves:** Choose a real-world zero-sum scenario (e.g. two companies competing for market share). Predict how each side might act and devise a strategy that one side could use to outmaneuver the other.

Key Takeaway

Zero-sum games are defined by competition, not collaboration. Mastering these situations requires sharp tactics, anticipation, and an unwavering focus on maximizing your gains while minimizing your opponent's.

Chapter 7: Non-Zero-Sum Games – Shared Triumphs through Working Together

Why This Matters

Unlike zero-sum games, where one player's gain is another's loss, **non-zero-sum games** open the door to mutual success. These situations represent the reality of most human interactions: cooperation can create outcomes where everyone benefits, and competition is not always necessary.

The foundation of non-zero-sum games was first explored by John von Neumann and Oskar Morgenstern in their groundbreaking work *Theory of Games and Economic Behavior* (1944). Later, Robert Axelrod's research on cooperative strategies in *The Evolution of Cooperation* (1984) demonstrated how reciprocity and mutual benefit drive success in these scenarios.

Non-zero-sum dynamics are found everywhere—from business partnerships to global climate agreements. Understanding how to navigate these scenarios enables you to focus on building alliances, sharing resources, and pursuing outcomes that grow the total "pie" instead of fighting over limited slices.

Mastering non-zero-sum games changes how you approach relationships, negotiations, and problem-solving. Instead of seeing others as rivals, you'll learn to identify opportunities for collaboration, even in competitive settings. This mindset fosters creativity, trust, and long-term success.

How It Works

Non-zero-sum games occur when the total benefits available can grow through cooperation. A classic example is trade: two nations can exchange goods and services to improve their overall economic well-being, rather than competing over limited resources.

Elinor Ostrom, in her work *Governing the Commons* (2010), showed how groups that cooperatively manage shared resources, such as water or fisheries, often achieve non-zero-sum outcomes. By establishing trust and clear communication, these groups increase the overall value of their shared assets, benefiting everyone involved.

Consider a scenario where two companies operate in overlapping markets. Instead of undercutting each other on price (zero-sum behavior), they could collaborate to create complementary products, driving overall demand higher. This approach benefits both parties, as well as their customers.

The key to non-zero-sum games is recognizing interdependence. Success often relies on building trust, aligning incentives, and communicating effectively. However, these scenarios can also involve risks — if one side defects or betrays the agreement, mutual benefits collapse. Thus, managing trust and incentives becomes critical.

Real-Life Example

A powerful example of a non-zero-sum game is the Paris Climate Agreement. Countries worldwide agreed to reduce greenhouse gas emissions for the benefit of the planet. By cooperating, nations collectively address a global threat, creating a safer environment for future generations.

However, this collaboration requires trust. If one country "defects" by failing to meet its commitments, others may lose faith and withdraw. The agreement succeeds only when all parties work toward the shared goal. This dynamic highlights the potential — and fragility — of non-zero-sum games.

On a smaller scale, imagine two rival coffee shops on the same street. Instead of battling over customers, they could partner to organize a neighborhood coffee festival, attracting more visitors to the area. By working together, they create a win-win situation, increasing their profits and community engagement.

Exercises

1. **Identify Non-Zero-Sum Opportunities:** Think of a current challenge in your life where you see competition (e.g. at work or in your community). Write down one way collaboration with others could create mutual benefits.

2. **Analyze a Partnership:** Choose a famous business or political partnership (e.g. Apple and app developers, or international trade agreements). How does it represent a non-zero-sum game? What risks and benefits were involved?

3. **Simulate Cooperation:** With a friend, design a simple non-zero-sum game (e.g. combining resources to complete a task). Track how your strategies evolve as you work toward maximizing shared outcomes.

Key Takeaway

Non-zero-sum games reveal that success doesn't always require defeating others. By fostering collaboration, building trust, and aligning goals, you can create outcomes where everyone benefits — a hallmark of strategic and creative thinking.

Chapter 8: Backward Induction – Thinking Ahead, Acting Backward

Why This Matters

Some decisions require thinking far into the future, but planning ahead without a clear process can feel overwhelming. Backward induction, a key principle of game theory, provides a structured way to navigate complex scenarios. By starting with your desired outcome and working backward, you can create a roadmap that guides your present actions.

This method is invaluable in sequential games, where one player's move influences the next. Backward induction ensures that every step aligns with your long-term goals, whether you're negotiating, strategizing, or solving everyday challenges. As John von Neumann and Oskar Morgenstern demonstrated in *Theory of Games and Economic Behavior* (1944), backward induction is a cornerstone for solving sequential games where foresight is essential.

In real life, backward induction matters because it prevents you from being blindsided by short-term obstacles. It's the key to anticipating challenges, managing resources wisely, and always staying one step ahead.

How It Works

Backward induction works by analyzing the final stage of a decision-making process and identifying the best choice at that point. Once the optimal outcome is clear, you move one step back and determine what decision will lead you there. This process continues until you reach the starting point, giving you a complete plan from beginning to end.

For example, in chess, a skilled player doesn't just focus on their next move—they visualize the endgame and work backward to determine the sequence of moves that will achieve victory. Similarly, backward induction is used in negotiations to anticipate the other party's final position and adjust your approach in earlier stages to steer the outcome in your favor.

Robert Gibbons' *A Primer in Game Theory* (1992) explains how backward induction is especially useful in dynamic scenarios, such as auctions or project planning, where each decision builds on the previous one. It helps players avoid reactive choices by focusing on the big picture.

Real-Life Example

Backward induction is commonly used in the world of project management. Imagine a tech company planning a product launch. The desired outcome is to release a high-quality product on time. To achieve this, the company works backward:

1. Final stage: Product is launched.
2. Prior stage: Final testing and quality assurance must be completed.
3. Before that: Marketing materials must be ready.
4. Earlier stage: Core features must be developed and debugged.

Each step depends on the success of the previous one, so the team's decisions at the earliest stages are guided by their ultimate goal. If deadlines are tight, backward induction ensures resources are prioritized for tasks that directly impact the launch.

Another example comes from parenting. Imagine you want your child to develop good study habits by the time they reach high school. Using backward induction, you might start with the desired outcome—self-motivation—and work backward to implement earlier steps, such as introducing small, consistent study routines in elementary school and rewarding discipline along the way.

Exercises

1. **Plan Backward from a Goal:** Identify a personal or professional goal you want to achieve in six months. Write down the final result, then list the steps needed to get there, starting with the last stage and working backward to your present position.

2. **Apply Backward Induction to a Problem:** Think of a decision where multiple steps are involved (e.g. planning a vacation or managing a project). Use backward induction to create a plan and identify which initial actions are most critical.

3. **Analyze a Sequential Game:** With a friend, play a turn-based strategy game (e.g., tic-tac-toe or a card game). Practice using backward induction to predict your friend's future moves and adjust your current strategy accordingly.

Key Takeaway

Backward induction helps you think ahead by working backward from your desired outcome. By aligning your present actions with future goals, you can anticipate challenges, avoid short-term distractions, and create a clear path to success.

Chapter 9: The Stag Hunt – Risk and Reward in Collaboration

Why This Matters

Collaboration often requires trust, but what happens when that trust wavers? The Stag Hunt, a game theory concept dating back to Jean-Jacques Rousseau, explores this dilemma. It describes a situation where two players must decide whether to cooperate for a large reward (hunting a stag) or act alone for a smaller, guaranteed payoff (hunting rabbits).

The Stag Hunt teaches us how to weigh the risks and rewards of teamwork. If both players cooperate, they achieve a significant reward. However, if one defects and pursues a smaller gain, the cooperative effort collapses, leaving the other player worse off. As Brian Skyrms explains in *The Stag Hunt and the Evolution of Social Structure* (2004), this scenario provides profound insights into trust, risk, and the conditions required for successful collaboration.

In real life, Stag Hunt dynamics appear in business partnerships, team projects, and even international agreements. By mastering this concept, you'll learn when to trust others, how to reduce risks, and how to align incentives for mutual success.

How It Works

The Stag Hunt represents a coordination game where cooperation offers the highest payoff, but only if all participants stay committed. If either party abandons the effort, the outcome for the remaining participants is significantly worse than if they had pursued a smaller, individual reward.

Here's an example: Two hunters are in the woods. They can work together to catch a stag (a difficult task requiring full cooperation) or separately hunt rabbits (easier but less rewarding). The payoff matrix looks like this:

	Partner Hunts Stag	Partner Hunts Rabbit
You Hunt Stag	Large Reward (Cooperate)	No Reward (Defection by Partner)
You Hunt Rabbit	Small Reward (Self-Reliance)	Small Reward (Both Defect)

This structure mirrors real-world dilemmas where the best outcomes depend on trust and shared commitment. However, if there's uncertainty about the other party's intentions, players may default to the safer option, sacrificing potential gains.

Real-Life Example

Consider a start-up where two co-founders are deciding how to allocate their time. They can either focus on building a breakthrough product (the stag) or pursue smaller, less risky side projects (the rabbits). If both founders dedicate themselves to the product, they achieve ground-breaking success. But if one founder shifts their focus to a side project, the other's efforts are wasted, and the company falters.

The Stag Hunt's dynamics also appear in international relations. For example, nations working to combat climate change face a similar challenge. If all nations commit to reducing emissions (the stag), the planet benefits. However, if some nations defect by prioritizing short-term economic gains (the rabbit), global efforts weaken, and the cooperative goal fails.

Exercises

1. **Identify a Stag Hunt Scenario:** Reflect on a situation where you had to decide between cooperation and self-reliance. What factors influenced your choice? Did the outcome resemble a Stag Hunt dynamic?

2. **Simulate Trust in a Team Game:** Pair up with a friend and create a scenario where you can choose to cooperate for a large reward or act independently for a smaller, guaranteed payoff. Play multiple rounds and discuss how trust evolves over time.

3. **Evaluate Trust in Collaboration:** Think of a team project or partnership you've been part of. Analyze whether everyone stayed committed to the shared goal or if someone prioritized individual rewards. How did this affect the outcome?

Key Takeaway

The Stag Hunt illustrates the importance of trust and alignment in collaboration. By fostering shared commitment and reducing risks, you can achieve greater rewards through teamwork, even in uncertain situations.

References for Chapter 9

1. Skyrms, Brian. (2004). *The Stag Hunt and the Evolution of Social Structure.* Cambridge University Press.

2. Rousseau, Jean-Jacques. (1755). *Discourse on Inequality.*

3. Axelrod, Robert. (1984). *The Evolution of Cooperation.* Basic Books.

Chapter 10: The Ultimatum Scenario – Balancing Fairness and Self-Interest

Why This Matters

Negotiations often hinge on fairness. But what happens when one party offers a deal that seems objectively better than nothing yet feels unfair? The Ultimatum Game, first introduced by Werner Güth and colleagues in 1982, reveals that humans often prioritize fairness over pure self-interest. It shows how social norms, emotions, and perceptions of justice can override rational economic behavior (Güth, Schmittberger, & Schwarze, 1982).

The Ultimatum Game is a key concept in behavioral economics, where researchers like Daniel Kahneman and Amos Tversky have explored how fairness and framing influence decision-making. Their work demonstrated that humans are not purely rational actors; instead, fairness and reciprocity often dictate behavior, even when rejecting an offer leads to personal loss (Kahneman & Tversky, 1981).

Understanding the Ultimatum Scenario matters because it helps you navigate situations where emotions and perceptions of justice outweigh cold calculations. From salary negotiations to business deals, recognizing when fairness influences decisions allows you to craft proposals that others are more likely to accept—building trust and long-term relationships.

How It Works

In the Ultimatum Game, two players must divide a sum of money. The proposer suggests a split (e.g. 70/30), and the responder can either accept or reject the offer. If the responder accepts, the money is divided as proposed. If they reject it, both players walk away with nothing.

Güth et al.'s 1982 experiments revealed surprising results: offers below 30% of the total were often rejected, even though accepting them would leave the responder better off than receiving nothing. This finding contradicted traditional economic theory, which assumes that humans act purely rationally to maximize personal gain.

Further research, including Fehr and Schmidt's *Theory of Fairness, Competition, and Cooperation* (1999), expanded on this by showing that fairness considerations are deeply ingrained in human behavior. People are willing to sacrifice personal benefits to punish perceived greed or unfairness, even at significant cost to themselves.

These dynamics have real-world implications. For instance, in international trade agreements, if one nation offers terms that are perceived as exploitative, the other nation may reject the deal outright—even if both sides stand to gain. Similarly, in workplace negotiations, lowball salary offers often backfire because they undermine trust and goodwill.

Real-Life Example

Consider a freelance graphic designer negotiating a project fee. The client offers $500 for a job worth $1,000, citing budget constraints. While $500 is better than nothing, the designer rejects the offer because it feels exploitative, fearing it sets a precedent for undervaluation.

This scenario mirrors the Ultimatum Game: the designer prioritizes fairness and long-term implications over immediate financial gain. The client learns that lowball offers can backfire, forcing them to revaluate their approach to future negotiations.

On a larger scale, the Ultimatum Scenario plays out in mergers and acquisitions. When one company offers terms heavily skewed in its favor, the deal may fail—not because the other party wouldn't benefit, but because accepting such terms feels like conceding too much. Kahneman and Tversky's research highlights this rejection of perceived losses, even when the deal offers measurable gains (Kahneman & Tversky, 1981).

Exercises

1. **Analyze a Past Negotiation:** Reflect on a negotiation where fairness influenced the outcome (e.g., dividing responsibilities, splitting profits, or setting prices). Did one party reject an offer despite tangible benefits? Why?

2. **Simulate the Ultimatum Game:** Play the Ultimatum Game with a friend. Start with a sum of money or tokens and experiment with different splits. Track how often low offers are rejected and discuss how fairness influenced decisions.

3. **Apply Fairness to Strategy:** Consider a current negotiation or decision where fairness is a factor. Write down how you might balance fairness with your goals to create a proposal that's acceptable to all parties.

Key Takeaway

The Ultimatum Game demonstrates that fairness often trumps pure self-interest in decision-making. By understanding this dynamic, you can craft proposals that respect others' perceptions of equity, building trust and avoiding rejection.

Part 2: Advanced Tactics for Decision-Making

Building on the foundational principles of game theory, this section dives deeper into advanced strategies that refine your decision-making skills. These concepts go beyond simple choices, addressing the complexity of dynamic environments, strategic deception, and long-term planning. Whether you're navigating competitive markets, resolving intricate disputes, or simply making high-stakes personal decisions, the tactics in this part will equip you to anticipate challenges, leverage opportunities, and achieve optimal outcomes. Each chapter introduces cutting-edge strategies backed by mathematical theory and real-world applications, ensuring you are prepared for even the most complex scenarios.

Chapter 11: Mixed Tactics – Embracing Calculated Randomness

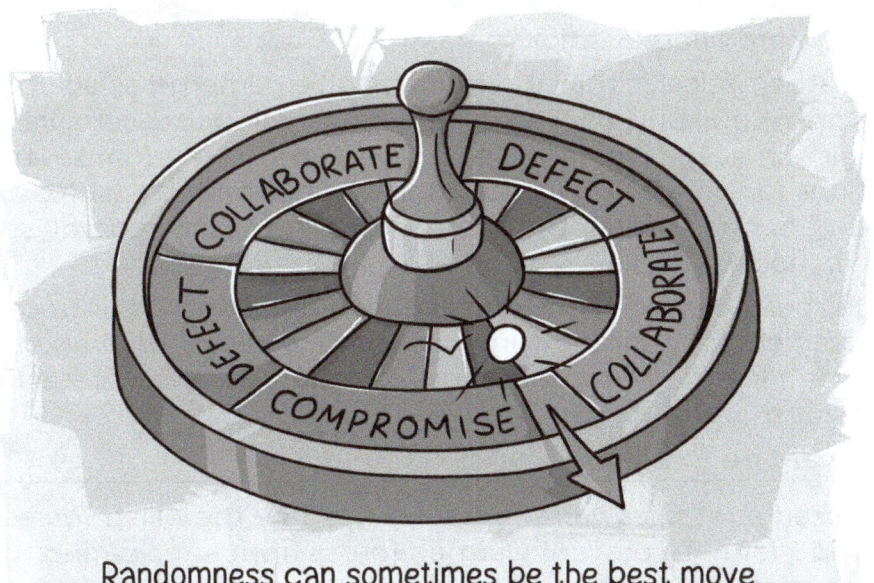

Randomness can sometimes be the best move.

Why This Matters

In highly competitive environments, predictability can be your greatest weakness. Opponents who can anticipate your actions gain an edge. This is where mixed strategies, a concept formalized by John von Neumann and Oskar Morgenstern in *Theory of Games and Economic Behavior* (1944), come into play. Mixed strategies involve introducing calculated randomness into your decisions to keep opponents guessing.

This approach is particularly relevant in zero-sum games, negotiations, and competitive industries. When your moves are unpredictable, you prevent others from exploiting patterns in your behavior. As explained by Roger Myerson in *Game Theory: Analysis of Conflict* (1991), mixed strategies are a powerful tool for achieving balance in scenarios where no pure strategy guarantees success.

How It Works

A mixed strategy involves choosing among multiple options with a specific probability distribution. For example, in a penalty kick during soccer, the kicker might randomly decide to aim left, right, or center, ensuring the goalkeeper cannot reliably predict their choice.

Mathematically, mixed strategies often emerge as solutions in Nash Equilibriums. For example, in rock-paper-scissors, no single choice dominates, so players must randomize their actions to avoid being exploited. This randomness ensures that each opponent faces the same expected payoff regardless of their choice.

In business, mixed strategies can be used to introduce unpredictability into pricing, product releases, or marketing tactics, keeping competitors off-balance and protecting market share.

Real-Life Example

Mixed strategies were famously used by the Allied forces in World War II. To prevent German forces from anticipating their troop movements, the Allies used deception and randomized tactics, such as false radio transmissions and decoy units, to disguise their true plans for the D-Day invasion. These tactics kept the enemy guessing, enabling a successful landing in Normandy.

In everyday life, mixed strategies apply to situations like negotiating salaries. For example, alternating between aggressive and cooperative approaches prevents the other party from establishing a reliable counter-strategy.

Exercises

1. **Simulate Randomized Choices:** Play a game of rock-paper-scissors with a friend, using randomization (e.g. rolling a die) to determine your moves. Observe how unpredictability affects the game's dynamics.

2. **Apply Randomness to Strategy:** Think of a negotiation or conflict where your choices have become predictable. Write down two ways you could introduce randomness into your strategy to regain the advantage.

3. **Analyze Randomized Business Tactics:** Research a company that uses unexpected moves to outmaneuver competitors (e.g. surprise product launches or flash sales). How does this randomness enhance their position?

Key Takeaway

Mixed strategies use calculated randomness to prevent opponents from exploiting patterns in your behavior. By embracing unpredictability, you can stay one step ahead in competitive and adversarial situations.

Chapter 12: Minimax Programs – Guarding Against the Worst-Case

Why This Matters

In uncertain situations, focusing solely on the best-case scenario can leave you vulnerable. The minimax strategy, a foundational concept in game theory, focuses instead on minimizing potential losses in the worst-case scenario. Originally developed by John von Neumann, the minimax approach is widely used in competitive environments, including chess, business, and conflict resolution (*Theory of Games and Economic Behavior*, 1944).

This strategy matters because it shifts your mindset to consider the worst possible outcomes and take proactive steps to mitigate risks. As explored in Luce and Raiffa's *Games and Decisions* (1957), minimax programs allow decision-makers to navigate high-stakes situations by prioritizing safety without sacrificing opportunity.

How It Works

The minimax strategy involves analyzing all possible outcomes and focusing on the one with the least favorable payoff. By choosing a move that minimizes your maximum loss, you create a safety net that ensures stability, even in worst-case scenarios.

Consider a simple example: A company is bidding for a contract. While they could offer an aggressive bid to maximize profits, this approach risks being undercut by competitors. Instead, using minimax logic, they might choose a moderate bid that reduces potential losses if competitors bid lower.

Minimax is particularly useful in zero-sum games, where one player's gain equals the other's loss. In such cases, preparing for the worst-case scenario ensures that your opponent cannot exploit your weaknesses.

Real-Life Example

The Cuban Missile Crisis of 1962 is a classic illustration of the minimax strategy. Facing a potential nuclear conflict, U.S. President John F. Kennedy and Soviet Premier Nikita Khrushchev both sought to avoid catastrophic outcomes. Kennedy's decision to implement a naval blockade, rather than launching a full-scale attack, minimized the risk of nuclear escalation while maintaining pressure on the Soviets. This calculated move exemplified minimax thinking, balancing assertiveness with caution to prevent the worst-case scenario.

In a business context, minimax is commonly applied in investment strategies. For example, portfolio diversification reduces the potential for catastrophic losses by spreading risk across different asset classes. Even if one investment performs poorly, the overall portfolio remains stable.

Exercises

1. **Apply Minimax Thinking to a Decision:** Identify a current challenge where the worst-case scenario could have significant consequences (e.g., launching a project, negotiating a deal). Write down the minimax strategy you could use to mitigate risks.

2. **Analyze a Historical Event:** Research a historical conflict or negotiation where leaders used minimax strategies to avoid disastrous outcomes (e.g., the Cuban Missile Crisis or trade wars). What steps did they take to guard against the worst-case scenario?

3. **Simulate a Game:** Play a zero-sum game like chess or tic-tac-toe. Focus on minimizing your losses rather than maximizing your gains. Reflect on how this approach changes your decision-making process.

Key Takeaway

The minimax strategy helps you guard against worst-case scenarios by prioritizing safety and stability in decision-making. By minimizing potential losses, you can navigate uncertainty with confidence.

Chapter 13: Commitment Devices – Strengthening Your Resolve

Why This Matters

In situations requiring decisive action, distractions or temptations can weaken your resolve. A commitment device eliminates alternative choices, forcing you to follow through on your decision. This concept, popularized by Thomas Schelling in *The Strategy of Conflict* (1960), demonstrates how removing options can strengthen your position and improve outcomes.

Commitment devices are essential for personal discipline, negotiations, and leadership. By limiting your future flexibility, you signal seriousness and prevent second-guessing. As explored in Elster's *Ulysses and the Sirens* (1979), commitment devices are like Ulysses tying himself to the mast: they ensure you stay focused, even when external factors try to pull you off course.

How It Works

Commitment devices work by creating constraints that lock you into a specific course of action. These constraints can be physical (e.g. locking your phone away to focus on work) or social (e.g. making a public declaration of your goals).

In game theory, commitment devices are powerful tools for shaping expectations and influencing others. For example, a company announcing an irreversible product launch date signals to competitors and customers that it's fully committed to delivering on time.

Real-Life Example

One famous example is Hernán Cortés' conquest of the Aztec Empire in 1519. Upon arriving in Mexico, Cortés ordered his ships to be burned, leaving no option for retreat. This dramatic commitment device motivated his troops to fight with greater determination, as failure meant certain death.

In everyday life, commitment devices are commonly used to achieve personal goals. For example, setting up automatic savings deductions from your pay check eliminates the temptation to spend, ensuring consistent financial progress.

Exercises

1. **Create a Commitment Device:** Identify a goal you've struggled to achieve (e.g. exercising regularly, saving money). Write down one commitment device you could implement to ensure follow-through.

2. **Analyze a Historical Example:** Research a historical leader or event where commitment devices were used to strengthen resolve (e.g. Cortés burning his ships). How did this strategy impact the outcome?

3. **Apply Commitments to Negotiations:** Think of a negotiation scenario where signaling commitment could strengthen your position. Write down the steps you could take to remove alternative options and enhance your credibility.

Key Takeaway

Commitment devices lock you into a specific course of action, removing distractions and demonstrating resolve. By eliminating alternatives, you can stay focused and signal strength in negotiations and decision-making.

Chapter 14: Schelling Points – Unspoken Agreements in Coordination

Schelling Point

Why This Matters

Coordination can be challenging when communication is impossible or limited. In such scenarios, people often rely on Schelling Points, or natural focal points, to align their actions. Introduced by Nobel laureate Thomas Schelling in *The Strategy of Conflict* (1960), Schelling Points explain how humans intuitively gravitate toward common solutions in the absence of explicit agreements.

This concept is essential for decision-making in uncertain environments, where clarity is scarce, and alignment depends on shared expectations. Understanding Schelling Points can help you predict others' behavior, solve coordination problems, and create strategies that leverage natural focal points to your advantage.

How It Works

A Schelling Point is a solution that people tend to choose in the absence of communication because it feels natural, special, or prominent. For example, if two people are told to meet in New York City without specifying a location, many will choose Grand Central Terminal because it's a well-known, central landmark.

Schelling Points emerge from shared cultural knowledge, geography, or intuitive reasoning. They can be used to solve coordination games where players must align their choices to achieve success. For example, if two companies want to set industry standards but cannot negotiate directly, they may both adopt widely used practices as the "natural" choice.

Real-Life Example

One famous application of Schelling Points occurred during the Cold War. Schelling himself analyzed nuclear deterrence strategies, noting how certain actions (e.g., stationing troops at critical borders) served as focal points for maintaining stability. These strategies sent clear, implicit signals to opponents without direct communication.

In a simpler example, think about splitting a restaurant bill among friends. Without discussion, people often default to evenly splitting the total, as it feels like the "fair" choice — a Schelling Point that avoids unnecessary debate.

Exercises

1. **Identify a Schelling Point:** Think of a situation where you coordinated with someone without explicit communication (e.g., choosing a meeting place or resolving a conflict). What natural focal point guided your decision?

2. **Simulate a Coordination Game:** With a friend, play a game where you must independently pick a number between 1 and 10. The goal is to match their choice without discussing it beforehand. Reflect on how shared knowledge or intuition influenced your choices.

3. **Apply Schelling Points Strategically:** Identify a negotiation or business decision where coordination is required. Write down one way you could use Schelling Points to align expectations or create agreement without direct communication.

Key Takeaway

Schelling Points help solve coordination problems by providing intuitive focal points for decision-making. By understanding and leveraging these natural alignments, you can navigate uncertainty and foster collaboration.

Chapter 15: Shapley Value – Fair Divisions in Complex Situations

Why This Matters

When multiple players contribute to a shared outcome, how do you fairly divide the rewards? The Shapley Value, developed by Lloyd Shapley in 1953, provides a systematic solution to this problem. It calculates each player's contribution to the overall success and ensures equitable divisions based on their input.

This concept is crucial in negotiations, resource allocation, and teamwork. By applying the Shapley Value, you can resolve disputes, design fair agreements, and foster trust in collaborative settings. Its mathematical precision ensures that everyone receives their due share, preventing resentment or feelings of unfairness.

How It Works

The Shapley Value assigns a value to each participant based on their marginal contribution to every possible coalition. Imagine three employees collaborate on a project, contributing different skills. The Shapley Value calculates the value added by each individual in various combinations, ensuring the reward reflects their unique contributions.

This method is widely used in cooperative game theory and real-world applications like profit-sharing, political coalitions, and even resource management. Shapley's approach ensures fairness while accounting for the complexity of group dynamics (*Contributions to the Theory of Games*, 1953).

Real-Life Example

Consider a start-up with three co-founders: one provides capital, another develops the product, and the third handles marketing. The company's success relies on all three, but their contributions are unequal. Applying the Shapley Value helps calculate each founder's fair share of profits based on the value they bring to the venture.

The Shapley Value also plays a role in international relations. For example, when countries collaborate on climate change initiatives, this method can help determine each nation's fair contribution to shared goals, balancing factors like GDP, emissions, and technological capabilities.

Exercises

1. **Calculate the Shapley Value:** Create a scenario with three contributors to a shared project (e.g. a group assignment or business venture). Assign values to their contributions and calculate a fair division using the Shapley Value formula.

2. **Apply Fairness in Real Life:** Think of a situation where you divided resources or rewards among multiple participants. How could the Shapley Value have guided a fairer allocation?

3. **Simulate Teamwork:** Form a group with friends and collaborate on a simple task (e.g. assembling a puzzle or brainstorming ideas). Use the Shapley Value to evaluate each member's contribution and decide how to allocate credit or rewards.

Key Takeaway

The Shapley Value ensures fair divisions by considering each participant's unique contributions. By applying this method, you can foster trust, resolve disputes, and create equitable outcomes in collaborative efforts.

Chapter 16: Bluffing and Signaling – The Art of Deception

Why This Matters

In strategic situations, the ability to mislead opponents or convey key information without direct statements can create a significant advantage. Bluffing and signaling are core tactics in game theory that help you manipulate perceptions, sow doubt, and force opponents to act based on incomplete or misleading information.

Bluffing and signaling are widely used in poker, negotiations, and even military strategy. As explored by Thomas Schelling in *The Strategy of Conflict* (1960), signaling allows players to send messages, whether truthful or deceptive, to influence others' decisions. Mastering these tactics enables you to disguise weaknesses, amplify strengths, and guide opponents into making suboptimal choices.

- **Bluffing:** Bluffing involves presenting false or exaggerated information to mislead others. In a negotiation, for instance, you might claim to have alternative offers to pressure your opponent into making a better deal.

- **Signaling:** Signaling involves sending credible messages, either truthful or calculated, to influence others' beliefs. For a signal to be effective, it must be costly or risky enough that it wouldn't be sent unless it were genuine. For example, a luxury brand signaling quality through high prices and exclusive marketing relies on the fact that low-quality brands couldn't afford the same tactics.

Bluffing and signaling are often intertwined. While bluffing works by exploiting uncertainty, signaling works by reducing it. Both require careful calibration: bluffing too aggressively risks exposure, while ineffective signaling fails to persuade.

Real-Life Example

In 1995, Microsoft famously bluffed its way into dominating the browser market. At the time, Netscape Navigator was the leading browser. Microsoft signaled its intention to develop a competing product — Internet Explorer — but exaggerated its readiness to launch, creating uncertainty for Netscape. The bluff forced Netscape to accelerate its development cycle, leading to rushed decisions and a loss of market dominance. Microsoft's actual product launch came later, but the psychological pressure they applied helped secure their position.

Bluffing and signaling also play critical roles in poker. For example, a player with a weak hand might bet aggressively to create the illusion of strength, forcing opponents to fold. Similarly, signaling appears in job interviews, where candidates use credentials, experience, or even attire to signal competence and reliability to potential employers.

Exercises

1. **Practice Bluffing:** Play a game of poker or a similar strategy game. Practice bluffing in low-risk situations to observe how opponents react. Reflect on how effective your bluffs were and why.

2. **Analyze Effective Signals:** Identify a product or service that uses signaling to convey quality or reliability (e.g., a luxury brand or a certification). How do these signals influence customer perceptions?

3. **Apply Signaling to Negotiations:** Think of a negotiation or decision where signaling could improve your position. Write down one way to use a credible signal to strengthen your case.

Key Takeaway

Bluffing and signaling are powerful tools for influencing perceptions and guiding opponents' decisions. By mastering these tactics, you can gain an edge in negotiations, strategy games, and competitive environments.

Chapter 17: Opportunity Cost – Recognizing What You Sacrifice

Why This Matters

Every decision involves a trade-off: by choosing one path, you inevitably forgo others. The concept of opportunity cost, first introduced by Friedrich von Wieser in 1914, helps you evaluate these trade-offs by quantifying the value of what you give up.

Opportunity cost is a vital tool for strategic thinking. As discussed in Mankiw's *Principles of Economics* (1998), it forces you to consider the unseen consequences of your choices and align decisions with your long-term goals. From financial investments to personal time management, recognizing opportunity costs ensures you don't waste resources on less valuable alternatives.

How It Works

Opportunity cost is the value of the next-best alternative you give up when making a choice. For example, if you spend $100 on dining out, the opportunity cost might be the savings or investment returns you could have achieved with that money.

In game theory, opportunity costs influence decisions in competitive and cooperative settings. A company deciding whether to invest in research or marketing, for instance, must weigh the opportunity cost of pursuing one strategy over the other. Opportunity cost also applies to personal choices, such as spending time on leisure versus skill development.

Real-Life Example

Consider a university student deciding whether to attend graduate school or enter the workforce. The opportunity cost of graduate school includes not only tuition fees but also the potential salary and career experience they forgo during their studies. Evaluating this trade-off helps the student make an informed decision based on their long-term career goals.

Exercises

1. **Calculate an Opportunity Cost:** Think of a recent decision you made (e.g., spending money, allocating time). Write down the opportunity cost of your choice. Was it worth the trade-off?

2. **Analyze a Business Decision:** Research a company's recent strategic move (e.g., a merger, product launch, or pivot). What opportunity costs might have influenced their decision?

3. **Apply to Personal Goals:** Identify a long-term goal you've been delaying. Write down the opportunity costs of continuing to delay versus starting now.

Key Takeaway

Opportunity cost highlights the hidden trade-offs in every decision. By evaluating what you sacrifice, you can make more informed choices and focus on the options with the greatest value.

Chapter 18: First-Mover Advantage – Leading for Personal Gain

Why This Matters

Timing can often determine the difference between success and failure. The first-mover advantage, a concept rooted in economic and strategic theory, refers to the competitive edge gained by being the first to act in a market or scenario. As explored by Lieberman and Montgomery in their seminal paper, *First-Mover Advantages* (1988), early movers can shape market dynamics, establish customer loyalty, and create barriers to entry for competitors.

This concept matters because it highlights how taking the initiative can set the stage for long-term success. However, the first-mover advantage is not guaranteed — without proper strategy, early entrants may falter, paving the way for competitors to capitalize on their mistakes. Understanding when and how to seize the first-mover advantage ensures you can act decisively and effectively.

How It Works

The first-mover advantage arises from several key benefits:

1. **Brand Recognition:** Being the first to introduce a product or service creates a lasting impression on customers, fostering loyalty.

2. **Resource Control:** Early entrants can secure valuable resources, such as patents, distribution channels, or prime locations, making it harder for competitors to catch up.

3. **Switching Costs:** By locking customers into their ecosystem, first movers create barriers to switching, further solidifying their position.

However, first movers face risks. As noted by Christensen in *The Innovator's Dilemma* (1997), pioneers often make mistakes that latecomers learn from, leading to a "fast-follower advantage." Success requires balancing bold action with careful planning to maximize the benefits of early entry while minimizing risks.

Real-Life Example

One of the most famous examples of the first-mover advantage is Amazon. Jeff Bezos founded the company in 1994 as one of the first major online retailers. By establishing an early presence in e-commerce, Amazon gained a dominant market share, built extensive distribution networks, and fostered customer loyalty. Even as competitors like Walmart and Target entered the space, Amazon's first-mover advantage allowed it to maintain leadership.

However, not all first movers succeed. Consider Friendster, one of the earliest social networking platforms. While it initially gained traction, technical issues and poor user experience allowed competitors like Facebook and MySpace to capitalize on its shortcomings. This example illustrates that being first is not enough — sustained success requires strategic execution.

Exercises

1. **Evaluate First-Mover Opportunities:** Identify a current industry or market trend where being the first mover could provide a competitive edge. Write down potential benefits and risks of acting early.

2. **Analyze a First-Mover Success or Failure:** Research a company that succeeded or failed as a first mover. What factors contributed to their outcome?

3. **Simulate Timing Strategies:** In a game or simulation (e.g. launching a product or entering a market), experiment with acting first versus waiting to observe competitors. Reflect on the trade-offs of each approach.

Key Takeaway

The first-mover advantage allows early entrants to shape the market and establish dominance, but success depends on strategic execution and the ability to adapt to challenges.

Chapter 19: Stackelberg Leadership – Dominating by Taking the Lead

Why This Matters

In many competitive scenarios, taking the lead enables you to set the tone, influence others, and shape the game to your advantage. Stackelberg leadership, named after economist Heinrich von Stackelberg, explores this phenomenon by analyzing how leaders and followers behave in sequential decision-making games (*Market Structure and Equilibrium*, 1934).

Stackelberg leadership matters because it provides a framework for understanding how to capitalize on being the first to act in structured environments. By taking the lead, you can force competitors to respond to your moves, gaining a strategic edge. However, effective leadership also requires anticipating how followers will react and ensuring your decisions remain optimal in the face of their responses.

How It Works

In Stackelberg games, the leader acts first, and the follower reacts based on the leader's decision. This sequence contrasts with simultaneous games, where players act at the same time. The leader gains an advantage by influencing the follower's choices, effectively shaping the outcome of the game.

For example, a dominant firm might set prices for a product, forcing smaller competitors to adjust their strategies to stay competitive. This ability to dictate the terms of the game makes leadership a powerful strategic tool. However, as noted in Fudenberg and Tirole's *Game Theory* (1991), the leader must carefully anticipate the follower's reaction to avoid unintended consequences.

Real-Life Example

Tesla exemplifies Stackelberg leadership in the electric vehicle (EV) market. By aggressively investing in EV technology, infrastructure, and branding, Tesla positioned itself as the industry leader. This forced traditional automakers to follow its lead, often playing catch-up in a market Tesla helped define.

Another example comes from sports. In a chess match, a player taking the lead by dictating the opening moves forces their opponent into a reactive position, gaining a psychological and strategic advantage.

Exercises

1. **Simulate Stackelberg Leadership:** In a strategy game or negotiation, take the role of the leader and make the first move. Observe how your actions influence others' responses and shape the outcome.

2. **Analyze Leadership in Business:** Research a company that acts as a leader in its industry (e.g. Apple). How do their early actions force competitors to adapt?

3. **Plan a Leadership Move:** Identify a situation in your life or work where acting as a leader could provide an advantage. Write down the steps you would take to influence others and achieve your goal.

Key Takeaway

Stackelberg leadership demonstrates how taking the initiative allows you to influence others and shape outcomes to your advantage. By anticipating reactions and planning strategically, you can dominate competitive scenarios.

Chapter 20: Sequential Interplays – Playing the Long Game

Why This Matters

Decisions made today often shape the outcomes of tomorrow. In sequential interplays, actions unfold over time, requiring players to think several steps ahead. Unlike simultaneous games where players act at the same time, sequential games involve anticipating future moves and counter-moves to maintain control and achieve long-term success.

This concept is vital in strategic planning, negotiations, and competitive environments where patience and foresight can secure significant advantages. Sequential interplays, as first modeled in *Theory of Games and Economic Behavior* by John von Neumann and Oskar Morgenstern (1944), reveal how structured decision-making over time can transform complex challenges into manageable steps.

As further explored by Fudenberg and Tirole in *Game Theory* (1991), sequential strategies rely heavily on the ability to anticipate responses. This requires not only logical planning but also a deep understanding of your opponents' incentives and constraints. Their work emphasizes that players who consistently evaluate future scenarios gain a distinct advantage in dynamic environments.

How It Works

In sequential games, players take turns making decisions, with each move influencing subsequent actions. These games often require players to evaluate potential outcomes at every stage, factoring in how opponents or collaborators are likely to respond.

The rollback method, commonly used in game theory, involves working backward from the desired outcome to determine the best initial move. This aligns with the principle of backward induction discussed in earlier chapters, but in sequential interplays, every step is part of a larger strategy.

Dixit and Nalebuff, in *Thinking Strategically: The Competitive Edge in Business, Politics, and Everyday Life* (1991), discuss how sequential strategies are not only about anticipating future moves but also about influencing those moves. For example, a company entering a new market might set prices aggressively low, forcing competitors to either accept reduced profits or exit the market altogether. By planning multiple steps ahead, the company shapes the competitive landscape in its favor.

Real-Life Example

A classic example of sequential interplays is the **U.S.-China trade negotiations**. Each country implements policies or tariffs in response to the other's actions, carefully evaluating how each step will influence the broader economic and political landscape. For instance, the U.S. might impose tariffs on specific goods, anticipating that China will respond with counter-tariffs. By thinking ahead, policymakers aim to guide the negotiation toward favorable terms without escalating the conflict unnecessarily.

In personal finance, sequential interplays appear in retirement planning. A young professional might choose to prioritize saving early in their career, understanding that the compounded returns from these savings will yield significant benefits decades later. Each financial decision builds upon the last, shaping their financial security over time.

Exercises

1. **Plan a Sequential Strategy:** Identify a long-term goal that requires multiple steps to achieve (e.g. career advancement, project completion). Write down the sequence of actions needed and consider how each step influences the next.

2. **Analyze Sequential Games in Politics or Business:** Research a political negotiation or business strategy where actions unfolded over time (e.g. trade wars, mergers, or international treaties). How did each party's moves shape the overall outcome?

3. **Simulate a Sequential Game:** With a partner, play a turn-based strategy game (e.g. checkers or a simplified negotiation). Focus on how your initial moves set the stage for future actions. Reflect on whether your strategy evolved as the game progressed.

Key Takeaway

Sequential interplays require thinking beyond immediate actions to anticipate and shape future outcomes. By planning strategically and evaluating each step's long-term impact, you can gain control over complex, time-dependent scenarios.

Part 3: Winning in Negotiations

Negotiation is both an art and a science, and mastering it requires strategy, preparation, and psychological insight. This section equips you with powerful tools to navigate negotiations with confidence and precision, whether you're closing a business deal, resolving a conflict, or making a life-changing decision. From understanding your Best Alternative to a Negotiated Agreement (BATNA) to leveraging the Anchoring Effect and manipulating time with the Deadline Master Plan, these chapters break down advanced tactics to give you the upper hand. Backed by game theory principles and real-world applications, these strategies ensure you'll negotiate from a position of strength and achieve mutually beneficial outcomes.

Chapter 21: BATNA – Always Have an Exit Plan

Why This Matters

The most successful negotiators are those who walk into a negotiation prepared to walk away. The Best Alternative to a Negotiated Agreement (BATNA) is your fallback plan if the deal on the table doesn't meet your needs. This concept, first introduced by Roger Fisher and William Ury in their seminal book *Getting to Yes* (1981), empowers negotiators by giving them clarity and leverage.

Max H. Bazerman and Margaret A. Neale expand on this concept in *Negotiating Rationally* (1992), emphasizing that a well-defined BATNA prevents emotional decision-making and reduces the chances of accepting unfavorable terms. By preparing alternatives in advance, negotiators create a solid foundation to assess offers objectively and protect their interests.

Having a strong BATNA matters because it shifts the balance of power. If you know you have a viable alternative, you won't feel pressured to accept unfavorable terms. Conversely, if your counterpart senses that you're reliant on the deal, they can exploit your vulnerability. By cultivating a strong BATNA, you can confidently reject bad offers and push for terms that meet your goals.

How It Works

Your BATNA is essentially your best fallback option. For example, if you're negotiating the price of a car, your BATNA might be another dealership offering a similar model at a competitive price. Knowing this gives you leverage: you can confidently walk away if the current negotiation doesn't meet your needs.

Fisher and Ury emphasize that identifying and strengthening your BATNA before entering a negotiation is critical. This preparation involves researching alternatives, assessing their feasibility, and determining the lowest acceptable terms you're willing to accept. Similarly, Bazerman and Neale highlight the importance of comparing your BATNA against the proposed terms during the negotiation process, ensuring your choices align with your broader goals.

Dixit and Nalebuff, in *Thinking Strategically: The Competitive Edge in Business, Politics, and Everyday Life* (1991), further illustrate how BATNAs can influence power dynamics. They argue that a well-communicated BATNA can subtly pressure the other party into making concessions, as they realize you are not dependent on the current deal. BATNAs are not just about walking away—they're about negotiating from a position of informed power.

Real-Life Example

Consider a job seeker negotiating their salary. If the candidate has another offer from a different company, they can use that offer as leverage. Knowing their BATNA (the alternative offer) gives them the confidence to push for higher pay or better benefits. On the other hand, a candidate with no alternatives may feel pressured to accept whatever is offered, regardless of whether it meets their expectations.

This principle applies in business as well. In 2011, Netflix raised its subscription prices, causing backlash and a wave of customer cancellations. Many customers who left had strong BATNAs: competitors such as Hulu offered comparable services. Bazerman and Neale argue that strong alternatives force companies like Netflix to reconsider their strategies, as customers are less likely to accept changes when viable substitutes are readily available.

Exercises

1. **Identify Your BATNA:** Think of an upcoming negotiation (e.g. salary discussion, business deal, or conflict resolution). Write down your best alternative if the negotiation fails. How can you strengthen this alternative before entering the discussion?

2. **Analyze a BATNA in Action:** Research a public negotiation or business decision where one party had a strong BATNA (e.g. mergers, strikes, or international trade deals). How did their BATNA influence the outcome?

3. **Strengthen Your Leverage:** Write down three ways you can improve your fallback options in a current or future negotiation. Consider resources, alternatives, or allies you can leverage.

Key Takeaway

A strong BATNA gives you the confidence to walk away from bad deals and negotiate from a position of power. By preparing your alternatives, you can ensure better outcomes and avoid being cornered in negotiations.

Chapter 22: Anchoring Effect – Setting the Tone Early

Why This Matters

The anchoring effect is a cognitive bias that heavily influences negotiations. It occurs when the first number or idea introduced in a discussion acts as a psychological anchor, shaping all subsequent decisions. Amos Tversky and Daniel Kahneman first explored this phenomenon in their ground-breaking work on cognitive biases, *Judgment Under Uncertainty* (1974), demonstrating how even irrelevant anchors can skew decisions.

Anchoring matters because the party who sets the anchor often gains the upper hand. A high opening bid can establish an expectation of value, while a low starting offer can reset the perceived range of acceptable outcomes. By strategically introducing an anchor, you can control the framework of the negotiation and subtly influence the final agreement.

How It Works

Anchoring works by planting a reference point early in the negotiation, which affects the other party's perception of value or fairness. For instance, if a seller starts by quoting a high price for a product, the buyer will unconsciously adjust their counteroffer relative to that initial figure — even if the price is inflated.

Tversky and Kahneman's experiments revealed that anchors are surprisingly sticky: even when participants knew the anchor was arbitrary, it still influenced their judgments. This effect is particularly powerful in negotiations because people often lack complete information and rely on the initial anchor as a guide.

In *Thinking Strategically* (Dixit & Nalebuff, 1991), anchoring is described as a tactical move to "frame the conversation," forcing your counterpart to play within the parameters you set. However, anchors must be chosen carefully. An anchor perceived as too extreme can backfire, undermining your credibility.

Real-Life Example

In real estate, anchoring plays a pivotal role. A homeowner selling their house might set an asking price significantly higher than the market average. Even if buyers negotiate the price down, the final sale price often ends up closer to the initial asking price than it would have if the seller had started lower. This tactic forces buyers to frame their offers relative to the anchor, often leading to higher outcomes for the seller.

Another famous example comes from retail sales. Stores often display a high "original price" next to a discounted price. Even if the original price was artificially inflated, it serves as an anchor, making the discount appear more significant and encouraging purchases. This phenomenon is rooted in Tversky and Kahneman's findings about how people assess value relative to anchors.

Exercises

1. **Practice Setting an Anchor:** Identify an upcoming negotiation (e.g. asking for a raise or selling a product). Write down a strong anchor you could use to set the tone early.

2. **Analyze Anchors in Business:** Research a business negotiation or pricing strategy where anchoring played a key role (e.g. mergers, salary discussions, or product pricing). How did the initial anchor influence the final outcome?

3. **Resist the Anchor:** Reflect on a situation where you were influenced by an anchor (e.g. making a purchase or negotiating a deal). Write down how you could have resisted its influence by focusing on objective criteria.

Key Takeaway

The anchoring effect demonstrates how setting the first reference point in a negotiation can shape the outcome. By strategically introducing an anchor, you can influence the perceived value and guide the conversation in your favor.

Chapter 23: Logrolling – Trading Concessions for Maximum Gains

Why This Matters

In negotiations, it's rare for both parties to value every issue equally. Logrolling is the art of trading concessions on lower-priority issues to gain advantages on higher-priority ones. By identifying each party's preferences, logrolling allows you to craft win-win solutions that maximize mutual gains.

This concept is extensively discussed in *Getting to Yes* (Fisher & Ury, 1981), where the authors emphasize focusing on interests rather than positions. Logrolling transforms negotiations from a zero-sum battle into an opportunity for creative problem-solving, ensuring both sides leave the table satisfied.

How It Works

Logrolling begins by identifying the issues at stake and ranking their importance. For instance, in a labor negotiation, management might prioritize cost savings, while employees prioritize better working conditions. By agreeing to concessions that matter less to you but more to the other party, you can secure concessions on issues that matter most to you.

Bazerman and Neale, in *Negotiating Rationally* (1992), highlight that logrolling requires trust and open communication. Both parties must reveal their true priorities, creating the transparency needed to identify mutually beneficial trade-offs. Successful logrolling often hinges on this collaborative mindset, ensuring no one feels exploited.

Real-Life Example

A classic example of logrolling occurred during the Camp David Accords in 1978. In negotiations between Israel and Egypt, facilitated by U.S. President Jimmy Carter, each side made concessions on issues of lesser importance to secure gains on their highest priorities. Israel agreed to withdraw from the Sinai Peninsula, addressing Egypt's territorial concerns, while Egypt recognized Israel's right to exist, fulfilling Israel's primary demand.

In business, logrolling frequently appears in vendor-client relationships. For example, a supplier might agree to faster delivery times (a priority for the client) in exchange for a longer-term contract (a priority for the supplier). By trading concessions, both sides achieve their goals.

Exercises

1. **Identify Logrolling Opportunities:** Think of a negotiation where you need to address multiple issues (e.g. work responsibilities, partnerships). Write down which issues are high, medium, and low priorities for you. How could you trade concessions to maximize gains?

2. **Research Historical Logrolling:** Study a major negotiation (e.g. international treaties or business deals) where logrolling played a role. How did the parties exchange concessions to achieve mutual benefits?

3. **Simulate Logrolling in Practice:** Role-play a negotiation with a partner where you have competing priorities. Practice revealing your preferences and trading concessions to find a win-win solution.

Key Takeaway

Logrolling is a powerful negotiation tool that turns conflicting priorities into opportunities for mutual gain. By trading concessions strategically, you can maximize outcomes and foster collaboration.

Chapter 24: ZOPA – Identifying the Zone of Possible Agreement

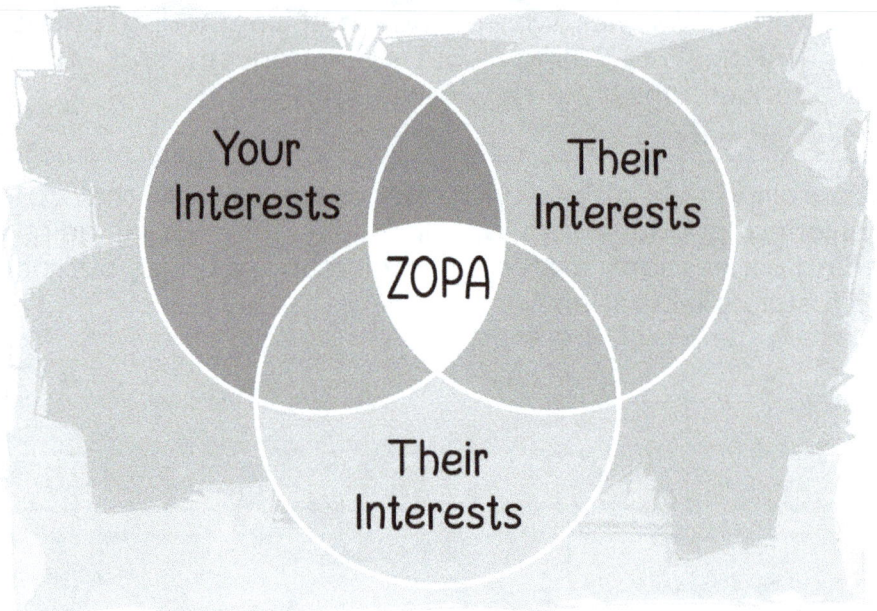

Why This Matters

Every successful negotiation depends on finding the Zone of Possible Agreement (ZOPA) — the range where both parties' interests overlap. First described in Fisher and Ury's *Getting to Yes* (1981), ZOPA is the space where deals are possible because both parties see value in the outcome.

Understanding ZOPA is critical because it prevents wasted time and frustration. If no overlap exists between the parties' acceptable terms, a deal cannot be reached. By clearly identifying ZOPA early on, you can focus your efforts on crafting agreements that satisfy both sides and avoid unrealistic demands that could derail discussions.

How It Works

ZOPA exists when the buyer's maximum willingness to pay exceeds the seller's minimum acceptable price. For instance, if a buyer is willing to pay up to $1,000 for a product and the seller is willing to accept no less than $800, the ZOPA is between $800 and $1,000. Negotiations within this range have a high chance of success.

In *Negotiating Rationally* (Bazerman & Neale, 1992), the authors emphasize the importance of preparation in identifying ZOPA. Both parties must understand their own limits (BATNA) and estimate the other side's limits to locate the overlapping range. Effective negotiators use probing questions and careful observation to clarify ZOPA during discussions.

Real-Life Example

ZOPA played a critical role in the 2015 Paris Climate Agreement, where nations negotiated emissions reduction targets. Developed countries prioritized limiting global temperature increases, while developing nations sought financial and technological support to transition to clean energy. The ZOPA lay in agreements that balanced environmental goals with economic development needs. This shared space allowed the parties to finalize a historic accord despite differing priorities.

In the business world, consider a software vendor negotiating a service contract with a client. If the client's budget is $50,000 – $70,000 and the vendor's acceptable range is $60,000 – $80,000, ZOPA lies between $60,000 and $70,000. Both parties can explore solutions within this range to maximize mutual value.

Exercises

1. **Define ZOPA in Your Negotiations:** Think of an upcoming negotiation. Write down your acceptable range and estimate the other party's range. Where do you think the ZOPA lies?

2. **Analyze a Historical Negotiation:** Research a high-stakes negotiation (e.g. international treaties, mergers). How did the parties identify and operate within the ZOPA?

3. **Role-Play a ZOPA Scenario:** Pair up with a friend and negotiate a mock deal. Each person should set their acceptable range privately. During the negotiation, identify where the ZOPA exists and close the deal within that range.

Key Takeaway

ZOPA represents the shared space where deals are possible. By identifying and operating within this range, you can negotiate effectively and avoid wasted effort on unattainable outcomes.

Chapter 25: Splitting the Difference – Mastering Compromise

Why This Matters

Not all negotiations end with one party getting everything they want. Splitting the difference is a widely used tactic to resolve disputes when parties are close to agreement but unable to settle on precise terms. By finding the midpoint between two positions, negotiators can break deadlocks and reach acceptable compromises.

Howard Raiffa, in *The Art and Science of Negotiation* (1982), explains that splitting the difference often works because it feels inherently fair to both parties. However, it's important to ensure the midpoint reflects a balanced compromise rather than a capitulation to unreasonable demands.

How It Works

Splitting the difference involves taking the average or midpoint of two offers. For example, if a buyer offers $9,000 for a car and the seller demands $11,000, they might agree to $10,000 — a straightforward compromise.

Fisher and Ury, in *Getting to Yes* (1981), caution against relying on splitting the difference too early. While it can resolve disputes quickly, it works best when both parties have made good-faith efforts to explore other options first. Otherwise, the resulting compromise might leave valuable opportunities untapped.

Real-Life Example

In labor negotiations, splitting the difference is a common strategy for resolving wage disputes. For instance, a union might demand a 10% raise, while management offers 5%. After prolonged talks, they might agree on a 7.5% raise. This midpoint ensures that both sides achieve partial success while avoiding a strike or impasse.

Another example comes from real estate. A seller might list their house at $300,000, while a buyer offers $280,000. Splitting the difference at $290,000 allows both sides to avoid further negotiation while securing a fair deal.

Exercises

1. **Practice Splitting the Difference:** Think of a recent disagreement (e.g. splitting costs or dividing tasks). Write down the positions of both sides and calculate the midpoint. Did this approach resolve the issue?

2. **Analyze When It Works Best:** Research a historical negotiation where splitting the difference was used (e.g. wage settlements or political compromises). Why was this tactic effective in that situation?

3. **Experiment with Alternatives:** Role-play a negotiation where splitting the difference is one possible solution. Explore other options first, then evaluate whether splitting the difference is the best choice.

Key Takeaway

Splitting the difference provides a simple, fair resolution when parties are close to agreement. However, it's most effective after exploring other options to ensure the compromise reflects genuine balance.

Chapter 26: Hardball Tactics – Standing Firm Against Pressure

This proposal really pushes that new software.

Let's check if the team pitching it has a stake in the company.

Why This Matters

Sometimes, negotiations become adversarial, and one or both parties resort to hardball tactics to gain an edge. These tactics can include high-pressure moves like ultimatums, take-it-or-leave-it offers, or even emotional manipulation. While hardball tactics can disrupt negotiations, understanding how to use them effectively—or counter them—ensures that you maintain control and protect your interests.

Hardball tactics are explored extensively in G. Richard Shell's *Bargaining for Advantage* (1999), where he outlines the principles of navigating high-pressure negotiations. Shell emphasizes that preparation, self-awareness, and composure are critical for neutralizing aggressive moves while maintaining a firm stance.

How It Works

Hardball tactics are designed to unbalance the other party, forcing them to make decisions under stress. Common tactics include:

1. **Ultimatums:** Setting a strict deadline or condition to force a decision.
2. **Good Cop/Bad Cop:** One negotiator takes a hard stance while the other appears sympathetic, creating psychological pressure.
3. **Highball/Lowball Offers:** Proposing extreme terms to anchor the negotiation and gain concessions.

In *The Power of Negotiation* by Harvard Business Review (2003), the authors argue that recognizing these tactics early is essential. The best counter-strategy is preparation: having a strong BATNA, staying calm under pressure, and reframing the conversation to neutralize aggressive moves.

Real-Life Example

In 1995, **the Major League Baseball strike** showcased the use of hardball tactics on both sides. Team owners attempted to impose a salary cap, while players threatened to walk out, knowing the financial losses would pressure owners to negotiate. Both sides used ultimatums, delays, and public pressure to gain leverage. Ultimately, while the strike disrupted the league, a new agreement was reached after both sides adjusted their tactics.

On a smaller scale, consider a landlord negotiating rent with a tenant. If the landlord issues a take-it-or-leave-it offer with a steep increase, the tenant might feel pressured to accept. However, a prepared tenant with alternative options (BATNA) could counter by citing market rates or negotiating for better terms.

Exercises

1. **Recognize Hardball Tactics:** Reflect on a past negotiation where hardball tactics were used against you (e.g., ultimatums, aggressive offers). How did you respond? What could you have done differently?

2. **Role-Play Resistance:** With a partner, simulate a negotiation where one side uses hardball tactics. Practice identifying and calmly countering these moves while maintaining focus on your goals.

3. **Develop a Neutralizing Strategy:** Think of an upcoming negotiation where you might encounter hardball tactics. Write down specific responses to common tactics like ultimatums or lowball offers.

Key Takeaway

Hardball tactics are designed to pressure you into making concessions, but they can be neutralized with preparation, calm responses, and reframing. Staying firm and focused ensures that you maintain control under pressure.

Chapter 27: Framing Effects – Shaping the Narrative to Win

Why This Matters

The way information is presented often matters as much as the information itself. Framing effects, a concept explored extensively in Tversky and Kahneman's *Judgment Under Uncertainty* (1974), demonstrate how decisions are influenced by how options are framed. Positive framing can make a proposal appear more appealing, while negative framing can deter undesirable choices.

Framing is critical in negotiations because it shapes the narrative and directs the other party's focus. By framing issues strategically, you can emphasize benefits, minimize drawbacks, and guide the discussion toward your preferred outcome. This aligns with insights from Heath and Heath's *Made to Stick* (2007), which highlights the importance of crafting messages in ways that resonate with others by focusing on simplicity, clarity, and emotion.

How It Works

Framing effects exploit the human tendency to evaluate options based on context rather than objective value. For example, framing a proposal as "saving $1,000" rather than "reducing a $5,000 loss to $4,000" makes the outcome feel more favorable, even though the net savings are identical.

In *Negotiation Genius* (Malhotra & Bazerman, 2008), the authors highlight that effective framing involves tailoring your narrative to the other party's values and priorities. Heath and Heath's research supports this by showing that messages framed around emotional or practical relevance are more likely to stick, influencing long-term decision-making and perceptions.

Real-Life Example

The Coca-Cola "New Coke" debacle of 1985 is a famous example of framing gone wrong. Coca-Cola introduced a new formula to appeal to modern tastes, framing it as an "improved" product. However, loyal customers felt this framing ignored their emotional attachment to the original formula, leading to widespread backlash. Coca-Cola quickly reverted to its original formula, demonstrating the importance of understanding your audience's perspective when framing decisions.

In personal negotiations, framing effects often influence salary discussions. For instance, framing a pay raise request as "aligning my compensation with industry standards" rather than simply asking for "more money" makes the request feel more reasonable and data-driven. This approach reflects the principles in *Made to Stick*, where Heath and Heath emphasize how framing ideas around clear and relatable contexts increases their persuasive power.

Exercises

1. **Practice Reframing:** Take a recent disagreement or proposal. Write down how you originally presented it and then reframe it to highlight benefits or align better with the other party's interests.

2. **Analyze Framing in Advertising:** Research an advertisement or marketing campaign. How does the framing influence perceptions of the product or service? Does it reflect any of the principles from *Made to Stick* (e.g., simplicity or emotional appeal)?

3. **Test Framing in Negotiations:** Role-play a negotiation where one person uses framing to influence the other party's decision. Evaluate how the framing shaped the final outcome.

Key Takeaway

Framing effects demonstrate that how you present information can significantly influence decisions. By shaping the narrative strategically, you can make your proposals more compelling and align them with the other party's priorities.

Chapter 28: The Decoy Effect – Steering Choices Subtly

Why This Matters

Sometimes, the best way to influence a decision is not by presenting fewer choices, but by adding a strategically designed one. The decoy effect, as explored in Dan Ariely's *Predictably Irrational* (2008), demonstrates how introducing a third option can nudge people toward a desired outcome.

The decoy effect matters in negotiations and decision-making because it leverages psychology to create perceived value. By adding an option that's less attractive but comparable to the desired choice, you subtly guide others toward the choice you want them to make. This strategy is particularly effective when the options involve trade-offs, such as price and quality. Daniel Kahneman's *Thinking, Fast and Slow* (2011) expands on this idea, emphasizing how intuitive (fast) thinking often dominates rational (slow) thinking, making people especially susceptible to relative comparisons like those in the decoy effect.

How It Works

The decoy effect occurs when one option (the "decoy") is intentionally included to make another option seem more attractive by comparison. For example, in pricing strategies, a retailer might present:

- Option A: $10 for a small popcorn.
- Option B: $15 for a medium popcorn.
- Option C (Decoy): $14.50 for a small popcorn.

Here, the decoy (C) makes the medium popcorn (B) appear like a better deal, even if the consumer wouldn't have considered it otherwise. Kahneman's concept of cognitive biases explains this phenomenon: people rely on fast, intuitive judgments when evaluating choices, and relative comparisons often dominate these quick decisions.

Richard Thaler, in *Nudge: Improving Decisions About Health, Wealth, and Happiness* (2008), also discusses the decoy effect as part of a broader toolkit for shaping decisions. By carefully designing choices, you can influence decisions without removing autonomy.

Real-Life Example

The Economist magazine's subscription pricing is a famous example of the decoy effect in action. At one point, the magazine offered these three options:

1. Online-only subscription: $59.
2. Print-only subscription: $125.
3. Online + Print subscription: $125.

The print-only subscription acted as a decoy, making the combined online and print subscription seem like a much better deal. This pricing structure increased sales of the combined option, even though the print-only subscription was never intended to be chosen.

Kahneman's work highlights why this approach is effective: people's intuitive (fast) thinking draws them toward the option that appears superior in a relative sense, without deeply analyzing whether all options are truly necessary or rational.

Exercises

1. **Design a Decoy:** Think of a decision where you want to influence someone's choice (e.g. offering a service package or presenting a business proposal). Write down two main options and a decoy that makes your desired choice more appealing.

2. **Analyze a Decoy in Action:** Research a product or service that uses the decoy effect (e.g. pricing strategies, subscription models). How does the decoy influence consumer behavior?

3. **Test the Decoy Effect in Negotiations:** Role-play a negotiation with a partner where you introduce a decoy option. Observe how it changes their perception of the other options.

Key Takeaway

The decoy effect is a powerful tool for subtly steering decisions. By adding a carefully designed option, you can influence choices and guide others toward outcomes that align with your goals.

Chapter 29: Supremacy Dynamics – Using Strong Points and Weakness

Why This Matters

Every negotiation involves a balance of power, and understanding supremacy dynamics — the interplay between strengths and weaknesses — can help you gain a decisive edge. This principle, rooted in Carl von Clausewitz's *On War* (1832), teaches negotiators to exploit their strengths while targeting the vulnerabilities of their opponents.

Supremacy dynamics are critical because they allow you to reframe power imbalances. Even if the other party appears stronger, understanding their weaknesses can level the playing field. This strategy involves not only leveraging your own assets but also carefully observing and capitalizing on gaps in their position.

How It Works

Supremacy dynamics involve two key tactics:

1. **Strength Maximization:** Highlight your unique advantages, such as expertise, resources, or alternatives, to establish dominance.

2. **Weakness Exploitation:** Identify the other party's pressure points—such as time constraints or dependencies—and use them to your advantage.

Clausewitz's ideas about targeting an opponent's "center of gravity" apply here. In negotiations, this might mean focusing on the key issue they care about most and using it as leverage. As Shell discusses in *Bargaining for Advantage* (1999), successful negotiators balance their strengths while probing for vulnerabilities, creating opportunities to shift the dynamic in their favor.

Real-Life Example

In the U.S.-China trade war, both countries leveraged supremacy dynamics. The U.S. used tariffs to target China's reliance on exports, while China exploited U.S. agricultural dependency to impose counter-tariffs. Each side identified the other's vulnerabilities while highlighting their own strengths, such as technological leadership or market size, to gain leverage in negotiations.

On a personal level, supremacy dynamics play out in job negotiations. A candidate with specialized skills (a strength) can demand higher compensation, while an employer facing tight deadlines (a weakness) might concede to those demands.

Exercises

1. **Identify Strengths and Weaknesses:** List your strengths and the other party's weaknesses in an upcoming negotiation. How can you use this information to gain leverage?

2. **Analyze Supremacy Dynamics in History:** Research a historical or business negotiation (e.g. the U.S.-China trade war). How did each side use their strengths and exploit the other's vulnerabilities?

3. **Simulate Supremacy Dynamics:** Role-play a negotiation where one party appears stronger. Practice using your strengths and targeting their weaknesses to level the playing field.

Key Takeaway

Supremacy dynamics involve leveraging your strengths and targeting the other party's weaknesses. By understanding the balance of power, you can create opportunities to shift negotiations in your favor.

Chapter 30: Deadline Master Plan – Using Time as Leverage

Why This Matters

Deadlines are not just markers of time — they are powerful tools for shaping negotiations. When used strategically, deadlines create urgency, pressure, and leverage, influencing how decisions are made. As explained in Richard Shell's *Bargaining for Advantage* (1999), deadlines force parties to act quickly, often leading to concessions that favor the more prepared negotiator.

Deadlines matter because they alter the psychological dynamics of negotiation. By imposing time constraints, you can steer discussions toward resolution, especially when the other party is unprepared to face the consequences of missing the deadline. This tactic works in both personal and professional contexts, from resolving business disputes to closing last-minute deals.

How It Works

Deadlines affect negotiations by introducing two key elements:

1. **Scarcity of Time:** As the deadline approaches, the pressure to reach a resolution increases. Parties are more likely to compromise to avoid the costs of a failed negotiation.

2. **Asymmetric Urgency:** If one party is more affected by the deadline than the other, the less-affected party gains leverage. For example, if a supplier is under pressure to meet a delivery schedule, the buyer can use that urgency to negotiate better terms.

Shell emphasizes that deadlines can be real (fixed and immutable) or artificial (created as a tactic). Artificial deadlines, when used strategically, can give the impression of urgency without locking you into a rigid timeline. Meanwhile, in *Negotiation Genius* (Malhotra & Bazerman, 2008), the authors highlight that successfully leveraging deadlines requires preparation and a clear understanding of both parties' priorities.

Real-Life Example

A well-known example of deadline dynamics occurred during the Brexit negotiations between the United Kingdom and the European Union. With hard deadlines looming for the UK's departure from the EU, both sides faced immense pressure to reach agreements on trade, border policies, and financial settlements. The EU, less affected by the looming deadlines, gained a strategic advantage, often forcing the UK to make concessions to avoid chaotic outcomes. This illustrates how asymmetrical urgency impacts negotiations when one side has more to lose from delays.

In everyday situations, consider real estate transactions. Buyers and sellers often face deadlines due to mortgage approvals, moving timelines, or market conditions. A seller with a strict deadline to close may accept a lower price to ensure the deal goes through, while a buyer under no time pressure can negotiate more assertively.

Exercises

1. **Analyze Your Deadlines:** Reflect on an upcoming negotiation or decision. Are there deadlines involved? If so, identify whether they are real or artificial and how they could be used to your advantage.

2. **Create an Artificial Deadline:** Design a negotiation scenario where you impose a deadline to create urgency. Observe how this changes the dynamics of the discussion and the other party's willingness to compromise.

3. **Research Deadline Tactics in History:** Study a major negotiation or event where deadlines played a critical role (e.g., Brexit, labor strikes, or high-stakes mergers). How did the presence of a deadline shape the outcome?

Key Takeaway

Deadlines are a powerful tool for creating urgency and driving negotiations to resolution. By understanding how time affects decision-making, you can strategically use or resist deadlines to gain leverage and control outcomes.

Part 4: Navigating Human Dynamics

The heart of decision-making lies in understanding people. Whether you're persuading, collaborating, or competing, mastering human dynamics gives you the edge. This section explores the psychological, social, and behavioral patterns that shape interactions. Armed with these strategies, you'll learn to anticipate actions, build trust, and navigate the complexities of group dynamics and individual biases. These chapters blend game theory, behavioral economics, and social psychology to help you master the human element in any scenario.

Chapter 31: Social Proof – Leading with Consensus

Why This Matters

Humans are inherently social beings, often looking to others for cues about how to think, feel, or act. Social proof, a concept popularized by Robert Cialdini in *Influence: The Psychology of Persuasion* (1984), explains how people are more likely to follow the lead of others, especially in uncertain situations. This psychological tendency can be a powerful tool in negotiations, marketing, and leadership.

Social proof matters because it creates momentum. When you demonstrate that others support your idea, product, or proposal, people are more likely to align with you, believing that the group consensus indicates credibility or value. However, as Cialdini warns, this tactic can backfire if the social proof lacks authenticity or relevance to the audience.

How It Works

Social proof operates on the principle that people tend to follow the crowd. For example, a restaurant displaying a "Most Popular Dish" label on a menu uses social proof to influence customers' choices.

Cialdini's research found that social proof is particularly effective in situations involving uncertainty or where people lack expertise. By highlighting examples of others adopting or endorsing a choice, you reduce hesitation and build confidence in your proposal. In *Yes! 50 Scientifically Proven Ways to Be Persuasive* (Goldstein, Martin, & Cialdini, 2008), the authors emphasize that tailoring social proof to match the audience's values enhances its effectiveness.

Real-Life Example

The Ice Bucket Challenge of 2014 is a prime example of social proof in action. This viral campaign encouraged participants to pour a bucket of ice water over themselves, post the video online, and challenge others to do the same—all while donating to ALS research. The campaign gained traction because participants highlighted celebrity involvement and displayed the growing number of people participating. As each new participant shared their video, the challenge's credibility and momentum grew exponentially, resulting in $115 million raised for ALS research.

This phenomenon aligns with principles outlined by Jonah Berger in *Contagious: Why Things Catch On* (2013), which emphasizes that visibility is key to social proof. The public nature of the Ice Bucket Challenge made participation visible to a large audience, creating a ripple effect of imitation and consensus.

Exercises

1. **Create Social Proof in Your Work:** Identify a project or proposal you're working on. Write down one way to use social proof, such as highlighting endorsements, testimonials, or group success, to build credibility.

2. **Analyze Social Proof in Action:** Research a campaign or movement that relied heavily on social proof (e.g. viral challenges, product launches). How did it influence behavior?

3. **Test Social Proof in Negotiations:** Role-play a negotiation where one party uses examples of others adopting similar terms to influence the other. Reflect on how this shapes perceptions of the proposal.

Key Takeaway

Social proof leverages the power of consensus to influence decisions. By showing that others endorse your ideas, you can build credibility and momentum, especially in situations of uncertainty.

Chapter 32: Contextualizing – Define the Rules to Trump the System

Why This Matters

Success in negotiations and strategy often depends not on playing the game better, but on redefining the game itself. Contextualizing involves framing or redefining the parameters of a situation to create favorable conditions. As discussed in David McRaney's *You Are Not So Smart* (2011), the way a situation is framed or structured heavily influences decision-making and behavior.

This approach matters because it allows you to take control of the narrative and the environment in which decisions are made. By setting the context, you establish the rules and priorities that others will follow, giving you a significant advantage.

How It Works

Contextualizing works by focusing attention on specific rules or framing that benefits you. For example, a salesperson might emphasize total value (e.g. "you'll save $1,000 over five years") rather than upfront costs, shifting the focus toward long-term gains.

In *Nudge* (Thaler & Sunstein, 2008), the authors explore how contextualizing — such as setting default choices or adjusting how options are presented — can guide decisions without restricting freedom. McRaney builds on this idea, arguing that people often fail to question the context, making it a powerful tool for influencing outcomes.

Real-Life Example

In 2003, Apple revolutionized the music industry by introducing the iTunes Store. At a time when music piracy via platforms like Napster was rampant, Apple reframed the rules of music consumption by offering an affordable, legal alternative. By contextualizing music as a digital asset rather than a physical product, Apple shifted consumer expectations and made purchasing individual songs for $0.99 an appealing option.

As highlighted in Walter Isaacson's *Steve Jobs* (2011), this reframing wasn't just about pricing; it was about reshaping how people viewed music ownership and access. Apple's contextual approach ultimately laid the groundwork for further innovations like Apple Music and Spotify, which expanded on the idea of digital access to transform the entire music industry.

Exercises

1. **Reframe a Proposal:** Think of a situation where you want to persuade someone. Write down the current framing and then redefine the context to highlight benefits that align with their priorities.

2. **Analyze Rule-Changing Strategies:** Research a company or leader who redefined an industry or negotiation rules (e.g. Tesla). How did contextualizing help them succeed?

3. **Test Contextualizing in Practice:** Role-play a negotiation where one party introduces new framing or rules. Reflect on how this changes the dynamics and outcomes of the discussion.

Key Takeaway

Contextualizing allows you to redefine the rules of engagement, creating an environment where success becomes more achievable. By shaping the narrative and structure of decisions, you gain a strategic edge.

Chapter 33: Moral Hazards – Avoid Incentivizing Bad Behavior

Why This Matters

A moral hazard arises when individuals or groups are incentivized to take risks because they know they'll be shielded from the consequences. Originally a term from economics, moral hazards now appear in negotiations, management, and policymaking. As Kenneth Arrow discussed in *The Limits of Organization* (1974), moral hazards stem from asymmetry between who bears the risk and who reaps the rewards.

Understanding moral hazards is critical because failing to address them can lead to irresponsible behavior, inflated risks, and systemic breakdowns. By carefully aligning incentives and accountability, you can create systems that encourage responsible decision-making without fostering recklessness.

How It Works

Moral hazards often emerge when people are insulated from the consequences of their actions. For example, employees with guaranteed job security might put in less effort if they know poor performance won't result in termination.

In *Thinking Strategically* (Dixit & Nalebuff, 1991), the authors emphasize that addressing moral hazards requires a balance of trust and incentives. Effective solutions include tying rewards to outcomes, improving transparency, and ensuring accountability. These measures realign the relationship between risks and rewards, mitigating reckless behavior.

Real-Life Example

The 2008 global financial crisis is a textbook example of moral hazard. Banks and financial institutions engaged in risky lending practices, knowing that potential losses would be mitigated by government bailouts. This lack of accountability incentivized short-term profits over long-term stability. As Joseph Stiglitz discusses in *Freefall: America, Free Markets, and the Sinking of the World Economy* (2010), moral hazards at multiple levels of the financial system contributed to the collapse, highlighting the dangers of shielding entities from the consequences of their actions.

On a smaller scale, moral hazards can arise in insurance. For instance, a car owner with comprehensive coverage might drive less cautiously, knowing that the insurance company will cover damages. This disconnect between responsibility and consequences leads to riskier behavior.

Exercises

1. **Identify a Moral Hazard:** Reflect on a system or process you're part of (e.g., workplace policies or shared resources). Are there safeguards that unintentionally incentivize risky or irresponsible behavior?

2. **Analyze a Historical Event:** Research the 2008 financial crisis or another event influenced by moral hazards. What were the misaligned incentives, and how could they have been addressed?

3. **Design an Incentive System:** Think of a scenario where you manage a team or resources. Write down how you would structure accountability and rewards to minimize moral hazards.

Key Takeaway

Moral hazards occur when people are shielded from the consequences of their actions, encouraging reckless behavior. By aligning risks and rewards, you can create systems that promote responsibility and accountability.

Chapter 34: The Tragedy of the Commons – Protecting Shared Resources

Why This Matters

The Tragedy of the Commons, first articulated by Garrett Hardin in his 1968 essay, describes how shared resources are often overused and depleted because individuals act in their own self-interest. This phenomenon appears in environmental issues, organizational settings, and even personal relationships.

Addressing the Tragedy of the Commons is crucial because it helps prevent the collapse of systems dependent on shared resources. Whether managing team projects, public goods, or ecosystems, understanding this dynamic enables you to foster cooperation and sustainability.

How It Works

The Tragedy of the Commons occurs when individuals prioritize personal gain over collective well-being, leading to resource depletion. For example, if a company overuses a shared data server for its own projects, it slows down performance for everyone else.

Hardin emphasized that solutions require collective action, such as setting usage limits, implementing penalties, or assigning property rights. Ostrom's *Governing the Commons* (1990) expanded on this idea, showing how communities can create successful resource management systems through cooperation, trust, and clearly defined rules.

Real-Life Example

Overfishing in international waters illustrates the Tragedy of the Commons. Without enforced limits, fishing companies exploit shared oceans, depleting fish stocks and harming the global food supply. Efforts like the United Nations Fish Stocks Agreement (1995) aim to regulate this behavior, but enforcement remains challenging.

In workplaces, shared resources like communal budgets or meeting rooms can fall victim to this dynamic. For instance, if one team monopolizes a shared conference room, others lose access, reducing overall productivity. Addressing such issues requires clear guidelines and collaborative planning.

Exercises

1. **Identify a Commons Issue:** Think of a shared resource you use regularly (e.g. office supplies, public parks). Are there examples of overuse, and how could this be mitigated?

2. **Study a Successful Solution:** Research a community or organization that successfully manages shared resources (e.g. water usage in arid regions). What strategies did they use?

3. **Propose a Policy:** Imagine managing a shared resource (e.g. a team budget). Write a policy to ensure sustainable and fair use.

Key Takeaway

The Tragedy of the Commons highlights the risks of overusing shared resources for personal gain. By fostering cooperation and setting clear rules, you can create sustainable systems that benefit everyone.

Chapter 35: The Sunk Cost Fallacy – Knowing When to Let Go

Why This Matters

The sunk cost fallacy is a cognitive bias that traps people into justifying further investments in time, money, or effort based on what they've already spent, even when it's no longer rational. This fallacy is a key concept in behavioral economics, popularized by Richard Thaler in *Misbehaving: The Making of Behavioral Economics* (2015).

Recognizing and avoiding the sunk cost fallacy is crucial because it allows you to make forward-looking decisions rather than being anchored by past commitments. Whether in business, relationships, or personal projects, understanding when to walk away can save you from throwing good resources after bad.

How It Works

The sunk cost fallacy occurs when decision-makers irrationally weigh previous investments, leading them to persist in failing ventures. For example, continuing to repair an old car that constantly breaks down might seem logical because of past repair costs, but buying a new car could be the more practical choice.

Thaler and Cass Sunstein, in *Nudge* (2008), emphasize that humans tend to overvalue past investments because of loss aversion — the fear of admitting failure or wasting effort. Breaking free from this bias requires reframing the decision in terms of future gains rather than sunk costs.

Real-Life Example

A notable example of the sunk cost fallacy occurred with Concorde, the supersonic jet project developed by Britain and France. Even after it became clear that the project was financially unsustainable, both governments continued funding it for years because of the significant resources already invested. This behavior exemplified the sunk cost trap, as described in *Behavioral Economics and Public Policy* (2014) by Camerer and Loewenstein, who argue that focusing on irrecoverable costs blinds decision-makers to better alternatives.

On a smaller scale, people often encounter the sunk cost fallacy in relationships. Staying in an unhealthy partnership because "we've been together for so long" exemplifies how past investments can cloud present judgment. Recognizing that sunk costs are irretrievable can help individuals prioritize future well-being over past efforts.

Exercises

1. **Identify Your Sunk Costs:** Think of a project, relationship, or habit where you've invested significant time or resources. Write down whether continuing offers future benefits or if it's time to let go.

2. **Analyze a Historical Example:** Research a business or government project that persisted due to sunk costs (e.g., Concorde or the Vietnam War). What lessons can be drawn from their decisions?

3. **Practice Reframing Decisions:** Imagine a scenario where you must decide whether to continue or quit (e.g., a project nearing failure). Reframe the decision based on potential future benefits rather than past investments.

Key Takeaway

The sunk cost fallacy traps decision-makers into irrational persistence by overvaluing past investments. By focusing on future benefits, you can make more rational and productive decisions.

Chapter 36: Information Asymmetry – Managing Knowledge Gaps

Why This Matters

Information asymmetry occurs when one party in a negotiation or decision-making process has more information than the other. This imbalance creates a power dynamic that can lead to unfair outcomes or strategic advantages. First articulated by George Akerlof in *The Market for Lemons* (1970), this concept is a cornerstone of economics and negotiation strategy.

Understanding and managing information asymmetry is crucial because it helps level the playing field. Whether you're the better-informed party or the one at a disadvantage, knowing how to use or overcome knowledge gaps can significantly impact the outcome of a negotiation.

How It Works

Information asymmetry often leads to two common outcomes:

1. **Exploitation:** The better-informed party uses their advantage to secure favorable terms (e.g., a car dealer selling a substandard vehicle to an uninformed buyer).

2. **Distrust:** The less-informed party, aware of the imbalance, becomes overly cautious, potentially derailing the negotiation.

Akerlof's research highlights that transparency and trust-building measures can mitigate these effects. In *Negotiation Genius* (Malhotra & Bazerman, 2008), the authors suggest techniques like sharing selective information, asking probing questions, and validating data to bridge knowledge gaps and build trust.

Real-Life Example

The used car market exemplifies information asymmetry, as buyers often lack the detailed knowledge sellers have about a vehicle's history. To address this, services like Carfax emerged, offering transparency through vehicle history reports. By reducing the information gap, these services have helped buyers make more informed decisions while encouraging sellers to provide higher-quality vehicles.

Another example comes from healthcare, where patients rely on doctors to interpret complex medical information. Mistrust can arise if patients suspect doctors of prioritizing profits over care. Efforts to improve transparency, such as offering second opinions or providing access to medical records, aim to reduce this asymmetry and foster trust.

Exercises

1. **Identify an Asymmetry:** Think of a situation where you were at an information disadvantage (e.g. purchasing a product or negotiating a contract). How did this impact the outcome?

2. **Analyze an Industry Solution:** Research a product or service (e.g. Carfax, online reviews) designed to reduce information asymmetry. How does it level the playing field?

3. **Practice Closing Gaps:** In a negotiation scenario, role-play as both the better-informed and less-informed party. Practice strategies like probing questions, transparency, and selective disclosure to manage the information gap.

Key Takeaway

Information asymmetry creates power imbalances in negotiations and decisions. By addressing knowledge gaps and fostering transparency, you can build trust and achieve fairer outcomes.

Chapter 37: Herd Behavior – Predicting Group Dynamics

Why This Matters

Herd behavior refers to the tendency of individuals to follow the actions of a larger group, often without fully considering their own information or judgment. This phenomenon, first studied in-depth by Banerjee in *A Simple Model of Herd Behavior* (1992), highlights how group dynamics influence decision-making.

Understanding herd behavior is crucial because it shapes markets, public opinion, and even personal decisions. From stock market bubbles to viral trends, recognizing when people are acting as part of a herd allows you to anticipate movements, avoid pitfalls, and strategically influence group dynamics to your advantage.

How It Works

Herd behavior arises when individuals prioritize group consensus over personal judgment, often to avoid standing out or making a mistake. For example, in a hiring decision, a manager might favor a candidate praised by others, even if they have reservations, simply to align with the group.

Banerjee's model shows how information cascades contribute to herd behavior. If early decision-makers act in a particular way, others are likely to follow, assuming the first group had better information. In *Thinking, Fast and Slow* (Kahneman, 2011), this tendency is tied to System 1 thinking — an intuitive, fast-response system — which seeks shortcuts in uncertain situations by deferring to the crowd.

Real-Life Example

The Dot-Com Bubble of the late 1990s is a famous example of herd behavior in financial markets. As investors saw others pouring money into internet start-ups, they followed suit, ignoring the lack of viable business models. This collective overvaluation led to an eventual market crash. Banerjee's analysis of herd behavior explains how the assumption that "everyone else knows something I don't" can lead to irrational mass decision-making.

On a smaller scale, herd behavior is evident in consumer trends. For instance, the rise of fidget spinners in 2017 saw millions of people buying the product simply because others were, rather than because of its intrinsic value. Understanding these patterns allows marketers to anticipate and even create trends by targeting key influencers within a group.

Exercises

1. **Identify Herd Behavior:** Think of a recent decision you made that was influenced by others (e.g., buying a product or choosing an activity). Was it based on personal judgment or the influence of the group?

2. **Analyze a Market Trend:** Research a market trend or bubble (e.g. cryptocurrency, NFTs). How did herd behavior contribute to its rise or fall?

3. **Simulate Herd Dynamics:** In a group decision-making exercise, have one participant act as an influencer by endorsing a specific choice. Observe how the group's behavior shifts and analyze whether the decision was rational or herd-driven.

Key Takeaway

Herd behavior drives group decisions, often overriding individual judgment. Recognizing and predicting these dynamics allows you to navigate or influence collective actions strategically.

Chapter 38: Reputation Capital – Building and Spending Trust Wisely

Why This Matters

In negotiations and decision-making, reputation is a form of capital that takes time to build but can be spent strategically. Reputation capital refers to the accumulated trust and credibility that influences how others perceive your actions and intentions. Axelrod's *The Evolution of Cooperation* (1984) demonstrates that a strong reputation encourages cooperation and deters adversarial behavior.

Reputation capital matters because it serves as both a shield and a bargaining tool. A trustworthy reputation earns goodwill, making others more likely to agree to your terms. However, reckless actions or broken promises can deplete this resource, damaging relationships and opportunities in the long term.

How It Works

Reputation capital is built through consistent behavior that aligns with shared values, honesty, and reliability. For example, delivering on promises strengthens trust, while failing to follow through erodes credibility. Axelrod's research shows that in repeated interactions, a good reputation deters exploitation because others value the benefits of continued cooperation.

In *Reputation Rules* (Diermeier, 2011), the author emphasizes that managing reputation involves balancing long-term consistency with occasional strategic risks. Spending reputation capital judiciously—such as calling in favors or challenging norms—can yield high rewards, provided it doesn't undermine future trust.

Real-Life Example

In the 1990s, Toyota built a reputation for reliability and quality through consistent product performance and customer service. However, a series of recalls in the late 2000s dented that trust. Toyota's response—open communication, accountability, and swift action—helped rebuild its reputation capital over time, demonstrating how managing credibility can sustain relationships even after setbacks.

On an individual level, professionals rely on reputation capital in networking. A manager known for integrity is more likely to secure promotions, partnerships, and loyalty from their team than one with a history of broken promises. This dynamic aligns with Axelrod's findings on reciprocity and trust in cooperative systems.

Exercises

1. **Evaluate Your Reputation:** Write down how others perceive your reliability, honesty, and collaboration skills. What actions could strengthen your reputation capital?
2. **Analyze Reputation Recovery:** Research a company or individual that successfully rebuilt their reputation after a crisis. What actions helped restore trust?

3. **Plan Reputation Spending:** Think of a scenario where you might need to "spend" reputation capital (e.g., asking for a favor or making an unpopular decision). How will you balance the immediate benefits with the long-term impact on trust?

Key Takeaway

Reputation capital is a valuable resource that builds trust and credibility over time. By managing and spending it wisely, you can strengthen relationships and achieve long-term success.

Chapter 39: Shadow of the Future – Decisions with Long-Term Consequences

Why This Matters

In repeated interactions or long-term relationships, the shadow of the future plays a critical role in shaping behavior. A concept explored in Robert Axelrod's *The Evolution of Cooperation* (1984), this principle explains how the anticipation of future encounters encourages cooperation and deters short-term exploitation.

Understanding the shadow of the future is essential for making decisions with lasting implications. In negotiations, business partnerships, or personal relationships, recognizing the long-term impact of today's actions helps you build trust, avoid conflicts, and foster sustainable outcomes.

How It Works

The shadow of the future operates on the idea that future consequences influence present behavior. For example, in a business partnership, one party might avoid deceptive tactics to maintain the relationship and ensure continued collaboration.

Axelrod's research shows that when players in a repeated game anticipate future interactions, they are more likely to adopt cooperative strategies like reciprocity. This principle also aligns with Elinor Ostrom's findings in *Governing the Commons* (1990), which highlight that long-term perspectives are critical for sustainable management of shared resources.

In practical terms, the shadow of the future creates accountability. Knowing that today's actions will impact tomorrow's opportunities encourages decision-makers to prioritize integrity, fairness, and mutual benefit.

Real-Life Example

The founding of the European Union (EU) is a compelling example of the shadow of the future. After World War II, European nations recognized that their long-term stability and prosperity depended on closer economic and political cooperation. The creation of the European Coal and Steel Community (ECSC) in 1951 laid the groundwork for the EU by fostering collaboration in industries critical to national security, reducing the likelihood of future conflicts. This forward-thinking approach prioritized shared, long-term benefits over short-term nationalism, ensuring decades of peace and economic growth in the region.

Exercises

1. **Evaluate Long-Term Impacts:** Think of a decision you're currently facing. Write down how it could influence your relationships, opportunities, or reputation five years from now.

2. **Analyze Cooperation in Repeated Games:** Research a successful partnership (e.g. between companies or countries). How did the shadow of the future encourage cooperation and deter exploitation?

3. **Simulate Long-Term Accountability:** In a role-playing exercise, negotiate a deal where future interactions are guaranteed. Observe how knowing you'll meet again influences trust, concessions, and decision-making.

Key Takeaway

The shadow of the future highlights the long-term consequences of today's decisions. By prioritizing sustainable, cooperative actions, you can build trust and strengthen relationships for lasting success.

Chapter 40: Overconfidence Bias – Avoiding Hubris in Planning

Why This Matters

Overconfidence bias is the tendency to overestimate one's abilities, knowledge, or control over outcomes. This bias, explored by Daniel Kahneman and Amos Tversky in their foundational research on heuristics, can lead to unrealistic expectations, poor planning, and avoidable failures.

Avoiding overconfidence is critical for effective decision-making. Whether in business, negotiations, or personal endeavors, recognizing your limits and accounting for uncertainty allows you to make more balanced, realistic plans. As highlighted in Kahneman's *Thinking, Fast and Slow* (2011), tempering confidence with critical thinking can prevent costly mistakes

How It Works

Overconfidence bias manifests in several ways:

1. **Overprecision:** Overestimating the accuracy of one's knowledge or predictions.
2. **Overestimation:** Believing one's abilities or outcomes are better than they are.
3. **Illusion of Control:** Assuming more influence over events than is realistic.

In *The Undoing Project* (Lewis, 2016), the partnership between Kahneman and Tversky demonstrates how overconfidence leads people to ignore warning signs, underestimate risks, and overcommit resources. Recognizing this bias requires incorporating feedback, consulting diverse perspectives, and preparing for worst-case scenarios.

Real-Life Example

The failure of WeWork's IPO in 2019 is a striking example of overconfidence bias. WeWork's leadership, particularly its CEO, overestimated the company's valuation, disregarded critical feedback, and failed to account for operational weaknesses. This hubris led to the collapse of the IPO and a drastic reduction in valuation, forcing a leadership overhaul and significant restructuring.

On a personal level, overconfidence bias often appears in career planning. For instance, someone might overestimate their qualifications for a job and neglect to prepare adequately for an interview, resulting in missed opportunities. Recognizing and addressing overconfidence ensures better preparation and adaptability.

Exercises

1. **Identify Overconfidence:** Reflect on a past decision where overconfidence led to a mistake. How could you have better accounted for risks or sought additional input?
2. **Analyze a Case of Hubris:** Research a business or leader whose overconfidence led to failure (e.g. WeWork, Blockbuster). What lessons can you apply to your own decision-making?

3. **Plan for Uncertainty:** In a current project, write down worst-case scenarios and how you would address them. Compare this approach to your initial expectations and adjust your plans accordingly.

Key Takeaway

Overconfidence bias blinds individuals to risks and limitations, leading to poor decisions. By recognizing this bias and accounting for uncertainty, you can make more realistic and effective plans.

Part 5: Resilient and Creative Strategies

Success in complex and ever-changing environments requires resilience, creativity, and the ability to adapt. This section explores strategies that equip you to thrive under pressure, plan for uncertainty, and turn challenges into opportunities. From building redundancy to prepare for failure, to leveraging a win-win mindset for collaboration, and mastering emotional regulation in high-stakes situations, these chapters provide actionable techniques to stay agile and forward-thinking. Whether you're managing limited resources, building coalitions, or practicing patience for long-term gains, this section emphasizes strategies that ensure sustained success in even the most dynamic circumstances.

Chapter 41: Redundancy – Preparing for Failure

Why This Matters

In any system, failure is not just a possibility — it's a certainty over time. Redundancy involves creating backup systems, resources, or strategies to ensure continuity and resilience when things go wrong. Nassim Nicholas Taleb highlights the importance of redundancy in *Antifragile: Things That Gain from Disorder* (2012), arguing that it acts as a buffer against uncertainty and unexpected events.

Redundancy matters because it protects you from catastrophic losses. Whether in negotiations, business planning, or personal projects, having alternatives and safeguards allows you to respond quickly and effectively to setbacks without losing momentum.

How It Works

Redundancy operates on the principle of distributing risks across multiple layers. For example, an entrepreneur launching a new product might maintain a reserve of capital to cover unexpected costs or have alternate suppliers to prevent delays.

In *The Checklist Manifesto* (Gawande, 2009), the author illustrates how redundancy — through simple yet systematic preparation — saves lives in fields like surgery and aviation. By anticipating potential failures and building safety nets, individuals and organizations can maintain stability even in crises.

Real-Life Example

The Apollo 13 mission of 1970 is a famous example of redundancy in action. After an oxygen tank exploded, putting the crew's lives at risk, NASA engineers relied on redundant systems and pre-tested contingency plans to ensure the astronauts' safe return. As Taleb notes, redundancy wasn't just a safety measure—it was the reason the mission didn't end in disaster.

In everyday life, redundancy can appear in personal finance. Maintaining an emergency fund ensures you're prepared for unexpected expenses, like medical bills or job loss. Without this safety net, a single crisis can create long-term financial instability.

Exercises

1. **Identify Redundancy Gaps:** Think about a current project or system you rely on (e.g. your work schedule, finances). What are the potential points of failure, and how could you create backups?

2. **Research Redundancy in History:** Study an event or project (e.g. Apollo 13) where redundancy played a critical role. How did the preparation ensure success despite failure?

3. **Plan Your Redundancy Layers:** Write down one area in your life or work where you could benefit from additional safety nets. Develop at least two specific backup strategies.

Key Takeaway

Redundancy is the foundation of resilience. By anticipating failures and building layers of backup, you can maintain stability and adapt effectively to unexpected challenges.

Chapter 42: Flexible Approaches – Adapting in Real-Time

Why This Matters

In rapidly changing environments, rigidity is a liability. Flexibility involves the ability to adjust plans, strategies, and mindsets in response to new information or shifting circumstances. As emphasized in *The Art of War* by Sun Tzu (translated 1910), adaptability is critical for survival and success, whether in battle, business, or negotiations.

Flexibility matters because static strategies often fail in dynamic environments. By staying open to change and reacting quickly to emerging challenges, you can seize opportunities, mitigate risks, and maintain momentum.

How It Works

Flexibility requires a balance between preparation and spontaneity. For example, a negotiator might enter discussions with clear goals but remain open to alternative solutions proposed by the other party.

In *The Lean Startup* (Ries, 2011), the author advocates for iterative approaches, where businesses continuously adapt their strategies based on customer feedback and market trends. This mindset enables rapid responses to change, reducing the risk of major failures.

Real-Life Example

The COVID-19 pandemic demonstrated the importance of flexibility across industries. Many restaurants adapted by pivoting to takeout and delivery services, while remote work became the norm for businesses worldwide. Companies like Zoom and DoorDash thrived because they quickly adjusted to meet new demands. As Ries suggests, flexibility allows organizations to turn crises into opportunities by aligning their actions with changing realities.

On a personal level, flexibility might involve adjusting career goals in response to economic changes. For instance, someone facing job loss might pivot to an entirely new industry, leveraging transferable skills to succeed in a different environment.

Exercises

1. **Evaluate Your Flexibility:** Think of a recent situation where your plans didn't work out as expected. How did you adapt, and what could you have done differently?

2. **Study a Flexible Organization:** Research a company that thrived by adapting to change (e.g., Zoom during the pandemic). What strategies enabled their success?

3. **Practice Flexibility in Decision-Making:** Simulate a negotiation where unexpected challenges arise. Practice adjusting your approach in real-time while maintaining focus on your goals.

Key Takeaway

Flexibility is the ability to adapt to changing circumstances while maintaining focus on long-term objectives. By staying open to new ideas and adjusting your strategies, you can turn challenges into opportunities.

Chapter 43: Scenario Analysis – Considering Through Every Outcome

Why This Matters

In a world filled with uncertainty, making decisions without considering possible outcomes can lead to costly mistakes. Scenario analysis is a strategic planning method that evaluates a range of potential futures to identify risks, opportunities, and contingency plans. Originating in military strategy and later adapted to business by companies like Shell in the 1970s, this approach allows decision-makers to act with foresight and confidence.

Scenario analysis matters because it helps you prepare for uncertainty. By anticipating how different factors might interact, you can build resilience against disruptions, make more informed choices, and avoid the paralysis of decision-making under pressure.

How It Works

Scenario analysis involves three key steps:

1. **Define Critical Variables:** Identify factors most likely to influence outcomes (e.g. market trends, competitor actions).

2. **Develop Scenarios:** Create plausible stories for how these variables might interact, such as "best case," "worst case," and "most likely case."

3. **Plan Responses:** Develop strategies tailored to each scenario, ensuring you're prepared no matter what happens.

In *The Art of the Long View* (Schwartz, 1991), the author emphasizes the importance of using scenario analysis not just for predicting the future, but for clarifying present uncertainties and strategic options. The method fosters creative thinking while grounding decisions in data and logic.

Real-Life Example

During the COVID-19 pandemic, hospitals used scenario analysis to prepare for potential surges in patient numbers. Administrators developed strategies for resource allocation based on different scenarios, such as "moderate increase in cases" or "overwhelming influx." This proactive planning allowed some institutions to manage resources effectively, avoiding critical shortages.

Businesses also relied on scenario analysis during the pandemic. For instance, airlines evaluated scenarios ranging from slow recovery to prolonged shutdowns, developing plans for each. Companies that engaged in thorough scenario planning were better positioned to adapt to unpredictable changes in travel demand.

Exercises

1. **Map Your Scenarios:** Identify a decision or project you're working on. Write down three scenarios — best case, worst case, and most likely case — and outline potential strategies for each.

2. **Analyze a Historical Example:** Research an organization or government that successfully used scenario analysis (e.g. Shell during the oil crisis of the 1970s). What lessons can you apply to your own decision-making?

3. **Simulate a Scenario Planning Session:** With a team or partner, choose a challenge and brainstorm possible outcomes. Develop plans for each scenario and discuss how they would impact your choices.

Key Takeaway

Scenario analysis prepares you to navigate uncertainty by considering multiple possible futures. By planning for a range of outcomes, you can make informed decisions and adapt to changing circumstances with confidence.

Chapter 44: Win-Win Mindset – Growing the Pie for Everyone

Why This Matters

A win-win mindset focuses on creating value that benefits everyone involved. First introduced in Fisher and Ury's *Getting to Yes* (1981), this approach emphasizes collaborative problem-solving to expand the "pie" rather than fight over fixed portions.

It fosters trust, creativity, and long-term relationships. When parties work together toward mutual benefit, they can uncover shared interests, resolve conflicts more efficiently, and create sustainable outcomes that satisfy all stakeholders.

Importantly, win-win strategies are not about being "nice" or making unnecessary concessions. As Covey explains in *The Speed of Trust* (2006), a win-win outcome is built on mutual respect and credibility, ensuring fairness while maximizing value for all parties. This approach requires clarity of goals, open communication, and a willingness to think beyond immediate, self-centered gains.

How It Works

Adopting a win-win mindset involves shifting away from competitive thinking and embracing collaboration. The process includes three essential steps:

1. **Separate Positions from Interests:** Positions are the surface-level demands people make (e.g. "I need a higher salary"), while interests are the underlying reasons behind those demands (e.g., "I need financial security"). By identifying and addressing interests, negotiators can find solutions that satisfy deeper needs rather than fixating on rigid positions.

2. **Generate Creative Options:** A win-win negotiation often requires thinking outside the box. Rather than framing a discussion as a single-issue conflict, such as "who gets more," negotiators can explore creative options that add value for both sides. For instance, in a job negotiation, instead of merely haggling over salary, the parties might consider additional benefits like flexible hours or professional development opportunities.

3. **Use Objective Criteria:** Disputes often arise from subjective perceptions of fairness. Using objective standards, such as industry benchmarks or market data, helps create a common ground for decision-making. This approach fosters transparency and reduces the risk of emotional conflict.

In *The Manager as Negotiator* (Lax & Sebenius, 1986), the authors stress that win-win solutions are particularly effective in complex, multi-party negotiations where shared goals can lead to exponential value creation. By reframing the negotiation as a joint problem-solving effort, parties can uncover opportunities that might otherwise go unnoticed.

Real-Life Example

The **Dayton Accords** of 1995, which ended the Bosnian War, exemplify the win-win mindset in high-stakes negotiations. Mediators focused on creating agreements that addressed the core concerns of all parties involved—territorial control, governance, and security guarantees—rather than forcing one side to "win" outright. By identifying shared interests, the accords achieved a fragile but lasting peace.

1. **Practice Separating Interests:** Think of a disagreement you've experienced. Write down the surface-level positions of each party and then list the underlying interests. How could a win-win approach address these interests?

2. **Analyze a Win-Win Negotiation:** Research a successful negotiation that used win-win principles (e.g. a high-profile business merger). What strategies fostered mutual benefit?

3. **Simulate a Collaborative Negotiation:** Role-play a negotiation where both parties work together to brainstorm creative options. Focus on expanding the "pie" rather than dividing it. Reflect on the outcomes and how they differ from a zero-sum approach.

Key Takeaway

A win-win mindset emphasizes collaboration and mutual benefit, transforming conflicts into opportunities to create value. By addressing shared interests, using creative problem-solving, and relying on objective criteria, you can achieve outcomes that satisfy all parties while fostering long-term relationships.

Chapter 45: Emotional Regulation – Staying Cool Under Fire

Why This Matters

Emotional regulation is the cornerstone of effective decision-making and negotiation. In high-pressure situations, emotions like anger, frustration, or anxiety can cloud judgment and lead to poor outcomes. As Daniel Goleman discusses in *Emotional Intelligence* (1995), the ability to recognize and manage emotions — both yours and others' — is a critical skill in leadership, negotiations, and conflict resolution.

Mastering emotional regulation allows you to think clearly, maintain focus, and respond constructively, even when tensions are high. It also prevents emotional outbursts that could damage relationships or derail discussions. This skill is especially valuable in complex negotiations, where composure often determines whether you secure a favorable deal or lose ground.

How It Works

Emotional regulation involves three key steps:

1. **Recognize Your Emotions:** Identify your emotional triggers and how they manifest (e.g. a racing heart, raised voice). Awareness is the first step in managing emotional responses.

2. **Pause and Reflect:** Take a moment to step back before reacting. Techniques like deep breathing or counting to ten can help defuse immediate emotional intensity.

3. **Reframe the Situation:** Shift your perspective to focus on the bigger picture or underlying goals, rather than the emotional trigger. This approach fosters constructive responses rather than impulsive reactions.

In *Thinking, Fast and Slow* (Kahneman, 2011), the author highlights how instinctive "fast thinking" often leads to emotional decisions. Emotional regulation helps activate "slow thinking," enabling more rational and measured responses.

Real-Life Example

Captain Chesley "Sully" Sullenberger's emergency landing on the Hudson River in 2009 demonstrates the power of emotional regulation in high-pressure situations. After a bird strike disabled both engines of US Airways Flight 1549, Sully remained calm and focused, quickly assessing the situation and executing a safe water landing that saved all 155 passengers and crew aboard. His ability to manage his emotions allowed him to think clearly, prioritize actions, and make life-saving decisions under extreme stress.

Sully's story is often cited as an example of emotional intelligence in action, aligning with Daniel Goleman's emphasis on self-control and composure as key components of effective leadership.

Exercises

1. **Identify Emotional Triggers:** Reflect on a recent situation where emotions influenced your actions. What triggered your response, and how could you have managed it better?

2. **Practice Calming Techniques:** Try a calming strategy like deep breathing, meditation, or visualization during a stressful moment. Record how it affected your ability to think clearly.

3. **Reframe a Conflict:** Think of a past conflict. How could you have reframed the situation to focus on solutions rather than the emotional trigger?

Key Takeaway

Emotional regulation allows you to maintain control and think clearly under pressure. By recognizing triggers, pausing before reacting, and reframing situations, you can respond constructively and achieve better outcomes.

Chapter 46: Empathy Mapping – Understanding Others' Motivation

Why This Matters

Understanding the motivations, fears, and desires of others is key to building trust, resolving conflicts, and influencing decisions. Empathy mapping is a structured tool for visualizing another person's perspective, helping you gain deeper insights into their mindset. As Simon Sinek explains in *Start with Why* (2009), understanding the "why" behind people's actions allows you to connect with them more effectively and align your strategies with their goals.

Empathy mapping matters because it transforms interactions. Whether negotiating, managing a team, or addressing a customer's needs, seeing the world from their perspective creates opportunities for collaboration, innovation, and influence. It also helps you anticipate objections and address them proactively.

How It Works

Empathy mapping involves answering key questions about the other person's experience:

1. **What Do They Say?** Understand their explicit concerns, demands, or feedback.

2. **What Do They Think?** Consider their beliefs, assumptions, or doubts that influence their behavior.

3. **What Do They Feel?** Identify emotional drivers like fear, excitement, or frustration.

4. **What Do They Do?** Observe their actions, habits, and decisions.

In *Designing for Growth* (Liedtka & Ogilvie, 2011), empathy mapping is presented as a tool to uncover hidden needs and align solutions with the other party's perspective. It helps you focus on understanding motivations rather than making assumptions.

Real-Life Example

Successful customer service teams often use empathy mapping to improve experiences. For example, Zappos, an online shoe retailer, trains employees to empathize with customers' frustrations, such as returning a pair of shoes. By focusing on the customer's perspective, Zappos consistently delivers exceptional service and builds lasting loyalty.

In negotiations, empathy mapping can be used to uncover shared goals. For instance, when negotiating a contract, understanding the other party's financial constraints or long-term objectives allows you to propose solutions that align with their priorities, fostering trust and collaboration.

Exercises

1. **Create an Empathy Map:** Choose someone you interact with regularly (e.g. a colleague, customer, or partner). Answer the four key questions to map their perspective and identify how you can address their needs.

2. **Analyze a Case Study:** Research a company or leader known for empathetic practices (e.g. Simon Sinek). How did empathy influence their success?

3. **Simulate Empathy in Negotiations:** Role-play a negotiation where one party uses empathy mapping to understand the other's needs. Reflect on how this strategy improves outcomes.

Key Takeaway

Empathy mapping provides a structured way to understand others' motivations, fostering trust and collaboration. By stepping into their perspective, you can anticipate needs, address concerns, and align strategies for mutual benefit.

Chapter 47: Asymmetric Warfare – Persevering with Fewer Resources

Why This Matters

In many situations, individuals or groups face opponents with significantly greater resources or power. Asymmetric warfare involves using unconventional strategies to counter these imbalances, turning perceived weaknesses into advantages. This concept originates in military strategy but is widely applicable in negotiations, business, and life. As discussed in *The Art of Strategy* (Dixit & Nalebuff, 2008), leveraging creativity and adaptability allows smaller players to succeed against formidable adversaries.

Asymmetric warfare matters because it teaches that resource limitations do not equate to inevitable defeat. Instead, those with fewer resources can focus on efficiency, innovation, and strategic maneuvering to achieve disproportionate outcomes. Whether you're a start-up competing with an industry giant or an individual negotiating with a large organization, understanding and applying asymmetric strategies can level the playing field.

How It Works

Asymmetric warfare relies on identifying and exploiting the vulnerabilities of a larger opponent. Key principles include:

1. **Leverage Agility:** Smaller players can adapt faster than larger, slower-moving opponents.

2. **Exploit Weak Points:** Identify areas where the larger entity is overextended, inefficient, or vulnerable.

3. **Focus Resources Strategically:** Concentrate efforts on areas where you can have the greatest impact, rather than spreading resources too thin.

In *The Innovator's Dilemma* (Christensen, 1997), the author highlights how smaller companies often disrupt industry leaders by focusing on niche markets the giants overlook. This principle of asymmetric strategy applies beyond business, emphasizing the importance of targeted, unconventional approaches to overcoming resource gaps.

Real-Life Example

The rise of Airbnb is a striking example of asymmetric strategy in business. Competing against established hotel chains with far greater resources, Airbnb leveraged a decentralized model, allowing property owners to offer accommodations without the overhead costs associated with traditional hotels. By focusing on underserved niches—such as travelers seeking affordable or unique experiences — Airbnb disrupted the hospitality industry, growing into a global powerhouse.

In personal contexts, asymmetric strategies can appear in job negotiations. For instance, a candidate without direct experience in a specific role might emphasize transferable skills, personal projects, or unique insights that larger, more experienced candidates might not possess. By shifting the focus, they can stand out and succeed despite lacking traditional qualifications.

Exercises

1. **Identify an Asymmetry:** Reflect on a situation where you faced a larger or more powerful opponent (e.g., a competitor, company, or team). How could you have used unconventional strategies to gain an advantage?

2. **Analyze a Disruptor:** Research a company or individual who succeeded against a more powerful competitor (e.g. SpaceX). What asymmetric strategies contributed to their success?

3. **Simulate an Asymmetric Challenge:** Role-play a scenario where one party has significantly fewer resources than the other. Practice developing creative strategies to overcome the imbalance.

Key Takeaway

Asymmetric warfare shows that resource limitations can be overcome with creativity, adaptability, and strategic focus. By identifying and exploiting vulnerabilities, smaller players can achieve outsized success against larger opponents.

Chapter 48: Coalition Building – Strength in Numbers

Why This Matters

Coalition building involves bringing together individuals or groups with shared interests to achieve a common objective. Whether in negotiations, activism, or business, coalitions amplify strength by combining resources, knowledge, and influence. This concept is central to game theory, as discussed in *Co-opetition* (Brandenburger & Nalebuff, 1996), where collaboration among competitors often creates more value than working alone.

Coalition building matters because it provides leverage in complex situations. By forming alliances, you can tackle challenges that would be insurmountable alone, amplify your voice, and pool resources to achieve collective goals. It also fosters diversity of thought, leading to more innovative and sustainable solutions.

How It Works

Effective coalition building involves:

1. **Identifying Shared Goals:** Find common ground among potential allies, even if your broader interests differ.

2. **Clarifying Roles:** Assign clear responsibilities to each member of the coalition, ensuring efficient collaboration.

3. **Balancing Contributions and Rewards:** Ensure that all parties benefit proportionally from the coalition's success, maintaining trust and commitment.

In *Getting to Yes* (Fisher & Ury, 1981), the authors highlight that coalitions work best when based on mutual respect and transparent communication. Avoiding hidden agendas and fostering shared accountability are key to sustaining partnerships over time.

Real-Life Example

The Civil Rights Movement in the United States exemplifies the power of coalition building. Organizations like the NAACP, Southern Christian Leadership Conference (SCLC), and Student Nonviolent Coordinating Committee (SNCC) joined forces with faith groups, labor unions, and student activists to push for civil rights reforms. Despite differing strategies and priorities, these coalitions united around shared goals, such as ending segregation and securing voting rights. Their combined efforts led to landmark achievements like the Civil Rights Act of 1964.

In the corporate world, coalition building appears in strategic partnerships. For example, car manufacturers and tech companies often collaborate to develop electric vehicles or autonomous driving technologies. These coalitions allow each partner to leverage the other's strengths, such as manufacturing expertise or software development, creating mutual benefits.

Exercises

1. **Form Your Own Coalition:** Think of a challenge or goal you're facing. Who could you partner with to combine strengths and achieve success? Write down their potential contributions and the shared goals.

2. **Analyze a Coalition in History:** Research a successful coalition (e.g. the Civil Rights Movement or a business partnership). What made their collaboration effective, and what challenges did they overcome?

3. **Simulate Coalition Negotiations:** Role-play forming a coalition with a group. Practice clarifying roles, balancing contributions, and maintaining trust throughout the process.

Key Takeaway

Coalition building demonstrates the power of collaboration in achieving shared goals. By uniting around common interests, balancing contributions, and fostering trust, coalitions can overcome challenges and create lasting success.

Chapter 49: Resource Management – Making Every Move Count

Why This Matters

In every aspect of life—whether in negotiations, business, or personal endeavors — resources are finite. Resource management is the art of allocating time, money, energy, or talent effectively to achieve maximum impact. As Peter Drucker emphasizes in *The Effective Executive* (1967), the way you use resources often matters more than the resources themselves.

Mastering resource management is crucial because even the most abundant assets can be wasted without a clear strategy. Conversely, individuals or organizations with limited resources can achieve remarkable results by optimizing their use. Whether facing tight budgets, constrained timeframes, or limited manpower, effective resource management ensures that every move counts.

How It Works

Resource management involves:

1. **Prioritizing Goals:** Focus on high-impact objectives that align with long-term strategies. Avoid spreading resources too thin by trying to achieve everything at once.

2. **Allocating Strategically:** Divide resources based on priority, urgency, and return on investment. For example, dedicate more funding to projects with clear potential for success.

3. **Monitoring and Adjusting:** Continuously evaluate how resources are being used and make necessary adjustments to stay on track.

In *Essentialism* (McKeown, 2014), the author emphasizes the importance of "less but better," focusing on a few critical priorities instead of attempting to tackle everything at once. This mindset is key to efficient resource management.

Real-Life Example

During the Battle of Thermopylae, King Leonidas of Sparta exemplified resource management by using a small force of 300 Spartans to defend against a much larger Persian army. By carefully choosing the narrow mountain pass as the battleground, Leonidas maximized his limited manpower's effectiveness, holding off the Persian forces far longer than expected. This tactical use of resources became legendary and underscores the power of strategic thinking in constrained situations.

In business, small start-ups often face resource constraints but succeed by focusing on their core strengths. For example, WhatsApp began with a small team but concentrated its efforts on providing a simple, efficient messaging platform. By managing their limited resources effectively, they grew into one of the most successful messaging services globally before being acquired by Facebook.

Exercises

1. **Prioritize Your Resources:** Think about a current project or goal. List your available resources and rank them based on their importance and impact. How can you reallocate them for better results?

2. **Study a Case of Resourcefulness:** Research a historical event or company (e.g. the Battle of Thermopylae or a successful startup) where limited resources were managed effectively. What strategies did they use?

3. **Simulate Resource Allocation:** Create a scenario where you have limited resources (e.g. time, budget, or manpower). Develop a plan to allocate them strategically to achieve your goal.

Key Takeaway

Resource management is the art of achieving maximum impact with finite resources. By prioritizing goals, allocating strategically, and remaining adaptable, you can overcome limitations and achieve success.

Chapter 50: Leverage Longevity – Practice Patience for Big Returns

Why This Matters

In a world that often prioritizes instant gratification, patience is an undervalued but powerful strategy. Leverage longevity means focusing on long-term goals and enduring short-term setbacks to achieve significant returns over time. As discussed in *The Compound Effect* (Hardy, 2010), consistent, small efforts accumulate exponentially when given enough time.

Patience matters because many of life's most significant successes — whether in business, relationships, or personal growth — are the result of sustained effort over time. By practicing persistence and resisting the temptation for immediate results, you can achieve goals that might seem unattainable in the short term.

How It Works

Leverage longevity operates on three principles:

1. **Think Long-Term:** Set goals that align with your broader vision, even if they require years to achieve.

2. **Stay Consistent:** Focus on small, incremental progress rather than seeking dramatic, overnight changes.

3. **Endure Setbacks:** Recognize that temporary failures are part of the journey and maintain resilience through adversity.

In *Antifragile* (Taleb, 2012), the author emphasizes the value of systems that improve over time through sustained effort and adaptation. This concept applies to personal and professional growth, where patience amplifies the impact of consistent work.

Real-Life Example

Warren Buffett's investment philosophy epitomizes the power of patience. Buffett's strategy involves identifying high-quality companies and holding onto investments for decades, allowing compounding to work its magic. This approach has made him one of the world's wealthiest individuals. His success underscores the value of thinking long-term and resisting the temptation to chase short-term trends.

On a personal level, longevity can be leveraged in skill development. For example, someone learning a new language or mastering an instrument won't see immediate results, but years of consistent practice lead to fluency or expertise. By staying patient and persistent, individuals achieve milestones that once seemed out of reach.

Exercises

1. **Set a Long-Term Goal:** Identify a goal that will take at least one year to achieve. Break it into smaller milestones and commit to consistent effort toward each step.

2. **Analyze Patience in Action:** Research a successful person (e.g. Warren Buffett) or project that benefited from long-term thinking. What can you learn from their persistence?

3. **Reflect on Past Efforts:** Think of a time when patience paid off for you. What challenges did you face, and how did staying consistent help you succeed?

Key Takeaway

Leverage longevity emphasizes the power of patience and persistence in achieving big returns. By focusing on long-term goals, staying consistent, and enduring setbacks, you can unlock exponential growth and success over time.

Part 6: Strategies for Handling Complexity

As decisions grow more intricate and variables multiply, strategies must evolve to manage complexity effectively. This section explores how to navigate challenging environments, from mastering multi-party negotiations to using Bayesian reasoning in uncertain scenarios. These chapters provide tools for controlling escalation, adapting to shifting rules, and blending competition with collaboration. With a focus on clarity and precision, you'll learn to simplify overwhelming situations, leverage behavioral insights, and build robust plans that thrive in dynamic contexts. These techniques turn complexity into an advantage, equipping you to excel in even the most convoluted scenarios.

Chapter 51: Multi-Party Negotiations – Managing Complex Group Dynamics

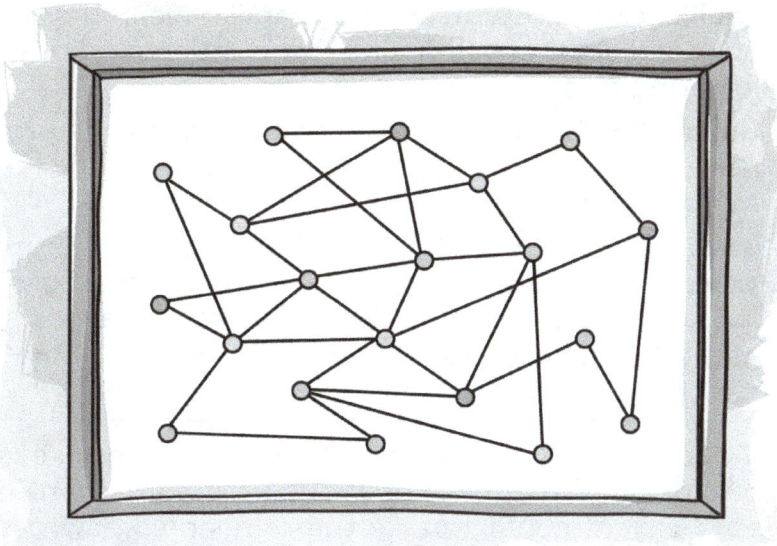

Why This Matters

Negotiations involving multiple parties are exponentially more complex than one-on-one discussions. Multi-party negotiations introduce competing interests, power imbalances, and the potential for coalitions, making coordination and consensus-building critical. As Howard Raiffa explores in *The Art and Science of Negotiation* (1982), managing multi-party dynamics requires clarity, strategic thinking, and the ability to align diverse objectives.

Mastering multi-party negotiations is essential because these scenarios often arise in high-stakes environments, such as mergers, policy-making, or international diplomacy. Successfully navigating them allows you to resolve conflicts, build consensus, and achieve outcomes that would be unattainable through unilateral action.

How It Works

Managing multi-party negotiations involves the following strategies:

1. **Clarify Objectives:** Identify and rank the priorities of all parties involved, ensuring transparency and alignment where possible.

2. **Facilitate Communication:** Establish clear channels for open dialogue, reducing misunderstandings and fostering trust.

3. **Build Coalitions:** Form alliances with like-minded parties to strengthen your position and create momentum toward a shared goal.

In *Getting to Yes* (Fisher & Ury, 1981), the authors emphasize the importance of focusing on interests rather than positions. This approach is particularly effective in multi-party settings, where creative solutions often emerge through collaboration.

Real-Life Example

The Good Friday Agreement of 1998 is a landmark example of successful multi-party negotiations. This agreement ended decades of violent conflict in Northern Ireland, known as "The Troubles." The talks involved multiple stakeholders, including the British and Irish governments, Northern Ireland's political parties, and various community leaders.

Negotiators overcame deep-seated mistrust by focusing on shared interests, such as peace and economic stability, while addressing core issues like governance and cultural recognition. U.S. Senator George Mitchell, who chaired the negotiations, used meticulous facilitation and ensured all voices were heard, demonstrating how clear processes and trust-building can bring diverse parties to a consensus.

Exercises

1. **Practice Mapping Stakeholders:** Think of a multi-party situation you're involved in or familiar with. Identify the key stakeholders, their priorities, and potential alliances. How could you build coalitions or find shared goals?

2. **Analyze a Multi-Party Negotiation:** Research a successful example of multi-party negotiations. What strategies were used to align competing interests?

3. **Simulate a Multi-Party Scenario:** Role-play a negotiation involving multiple parties with conflicting priorities. Focus on building coalitions, clarifying objectives, and achieving consensus.

Key Takeaway

Multi-party negotiations require aligning diverse objectives through clear communication, coalition-building, and shared problem-solving. By focusing on interests rather than positions, you can manage complexity and achieve meaningful outcomes.

Chapter 52: Design Approach – Setting the Stage for Success

Why This Matters

Success in complex situations often depends less on the actions taken during execution and more on the groundwork laid beforehand. The design approach emphasizes preparing the environment, participants, and processes to create conditions conducive to success. This proactive strategy aligns with Jeanne Liedtka's insights in *Designing for Growth* (2011), where she argues that thoughtful design fosters creativity, collaboration, and clarity.

The design approach matters because it allows you to shape outcomes before challenges arise. Whether leading a project, hosting a negotiation, or implementing change, setting the stage ensures smoother execution, minimizes friction, and improves outcomes.

How It Works

Applying the design approach involves:

1. **Define Objectives:** Clearly articulate what success looks like and ensure all stakeholders understand these goals.

2. **Plan the Environment:** Create a setting that fosters collaboration, such as neutral meeting spaces or structured agendas.

3. **Establish Processes:** Design frameworks for decision-making, communication, and conflict resolution to guide participants effectively.

In *The Art of Innovation* (Kelley, 2001), the author emphasizes how design-thinking principles, like prototyping and iteration, apply beyond product development to solving organizational and interpersonal challenges.

Real-Life Example

The Camp David Accords of 1978, brokered by U.S. President Jimmy Carter, showcase the power of the design approach. Carter created an environment conducive to peace talks by isolating Egyptian and Israeli leaders at the presidential retreat, removing external pressures, and fostering focused dialogue. His structured agenda and personal involvement helped secure agreements that had eluded years of open conflict.

Exercises

1. **Design Your Ideal Environment:** Think of a situation where you'll need collaboration (e.g. a meeting or negotiation). Write down how you would design the setting, processes, and communication methods to ensure success.

2. **Analyze a Designed Outcome:** Research a successful event or initiative (e.g. the Camp David Accords). How did its design contribute to its success?

3. **Test the Design Approach:** Apply the design approach to a small project or discussion. Reflect on how your preparation influenced the outcome.

Key Takeaway

The design approach ensures success by shaping environments, processes, and expectations before execution. By preparing thoughtfully, you create conditions that foster collaboration, innovation, and effective problem-solving.

Chapter 53: Bayesian Touchpoints – Playing with Incomplete Information

Why This Matters

In many decisions and negotiations, complete information is a luxury. Bayesian reasoning is a framework for making better decisions under uncertainty by updating your beliefs and strategies as new information emerges. Named after Reverend Thomas Bayes, this method is foundational in probability theory and decision science, as explored in *Thinking, Fast and Slow* (Kahneman, 2011).

Bayesian thinking matters because it helps you make informed decisions even when the facts are incomplete. By focusing on probabilities and continuously refining assumptions, you can navigate uncertainty with greater confidence and precision, whether you're analyzing market trends, negotiating deals, or responding to unpredictable events.

How It Works

Bayesian reasoning involves three steps:

1. **Set Prior Beliefs:** Begin with an initial estimate or assumption about the likelihood of an event or outcome based on available information.

2. **Incorporate New Evidence:** Evaluate how new data or observations align with or contradict your initial beliefs.

3. **Update Probabilities:** Adjust your beliefs accordingly, refining your understanding and improving your decision-making over time.

In *Superforecasting* (Tetlock & Gardner, 2015), the authors emphasize how expert forecasters use Bayesian principles to make accurate predictions. The key is maintaining flexibility and a willingness to revise your approach based on emerging information.

Real-Life Example

Medical diagnosis processes often employ Bayesian reasoning to refine conclusions with incomplete information. For example, when a doctor evaluates a patient with flu-like symptoms, they start with prior probabilities (e.g. it's flu season, making the flu a likely cause). As additional tests (e.g. temperature, bloodwork) are conducted, the doctor updates their assessment, ruling out other possibilities such as strep throat. This iterative process ensures decisions are guided by evidence and evolving probabilities, not assumptions.

Exercises

1. **Apply Bayesian Reasoning:** Think of a current decision where you have incomplete information. Write down your initial assumptions, then evaluate how new evidence might adjust your thinking.

2. **Analyze Bayesian Applications:** Research a system or organization that uses iterative updates, such as a recommendation engine or a weather forecast model. How does this process improve accuracy over time?

3. **Practice Real-Time Updates:** Role-play a negotiation where new information emerges throughout the discussion. Practice revising your approach as the conversation unfolds.

Key Takeaway

Bayesian reasoning helps you navigate uncertainty by continuously updating your beliefs based on new information. By staying adaptable and focusing on probabilities, you can make more informed and accurate decisions over time.

Chapter 54: The Value of Patience – Delaying Moves to Get Big Returns

Why This Matters

In a world driven by speed, patience is often underestimated. However, delaying action strategically can create opportunities for better outcomes. The value of patience lies in waiting for the right moment to act, gathering information, or allowing events to unfold favorably. As highlighted in *The Art of Strategy* (Dixit & Nalebuff, 2008), patience can turn seemingly minor advantages into significant wins.

Patience matters because rushing decisions often leads to missed opportunities or costly mistakes. By mastering the art of timing, you can increase the chances of success while reducing risks, whether negotiating contracts, investing in markets, or navigating personal challenges.

How It Works

The value of patience relies on three principles:

1. **Gather Information:** Use time to collect insights and reduce uncertainty before making a decision.
2. **Allow Momentum to Build:** Sometimes, waiting enables external factors to align in your favor.
3. **Control Emotional Impulses:** Patience requires discipline and the ability to resist pressure for immediate action.

In *The 48 Laws of Power* (Greene, 1998), the author highlights how waiting for the opportune moment is a key strategy used by influential leaders. Timing, when executed well, can amplify the impact of your actions.

Real-Life Example

Warren Buffett's investment strategy demonstrates the value of patience. Buffett famously avoids short-term speculation, instead waiting for undervalued companies with strong long-term growth potential. His patience has allowed him to make calculated investments that yield massive returns over decades, cementing his reputation as one of history's most successful investors.

In negotiations, patience can also turn the tide. For example, in real estate, a buyer might wait for a motivated seller to lower their asking price rather than rushing into a deal. This approach allows the buyer to secure a better value by letting circumstances evolve in their favor.

Exercises

1. **Identify a Situation for Patience:** Reflect on a current challenge where immediate action might not be necessary. How could waiting for the right moment improve your results?
2. **Analyze a Patient Leader:** Research someone known for their strategic patience (e.g., Warren Buffett). What lessons can you learn from their approach?

3. **Test Delayed Action:** Simulate a negotiation or decision-making scenario where one party waits for the other to act first. Reflect on how patience affects the outcome.

Key Takeaway

Patience allows you to maximize opportunities and reduce risks by waiting for the right moment to act. By gathering information, aligning external factors, and controlling impulses, you can make decisions with greater confidence and impact.

Chapter 55: Escalation Control – Avoiding Destructive Spirals

Why This Matters

Escalation is a common pitfall in conflicts and negotiations. When disagreements spiral out of control, they can lead to destructive outcomes, damaged relationships, and missed opportunities. Escalation control involves identifying and halting these spirals before they cause irreparable harm. As highlighted in *Getting Past No* (Ury, 1991), staying composed and redirecting the energy of a heated exchange can turn adversaries into collaborators.

Mastering escalation control is essential because unchecked conflicts drain resources, erode trust, and limit progress. Whether in professional negotiations or personal disputes, understanding how to de-escalate situations creates space for constructive dialogue and solutions.

How It Works

Escalation control involves:

1. **Recognizing Early Signs:** Identify when a discussion is becoming unproductive or overly emotional. Look for raised voices, rigid positions, or repetitive arguments.

2. **Interrupting the Cycle:** Use calming techniques, such as taking a break, acknowledging emotions, or shifting the focus to shared goals.

3. **Redirecting Energy:** Reframe the issue to focus on problem-solving rather than blame or competition.

In *Crucial Conversations* (Patterson et al., 2002), the authors stress the importance of creating a safe environment for dialogue. Escalation often occurs when people feel threatened or misunderstood, so fostering safety is key to regaining control.

Real-Life Example

The Montgomery Bus Boycott of 1955–1956 is a powerful example of escalation control in social movements. When Rosa Parks' arrest sparked outrage over racial segregation, civil rights leaders like Martin Luther King Jr. maintained a strategy of nonviolence and measured responses. Despite provocations and threats, the boycott avoided destructive escalation by focusing on peaceful protest, coordinated communication, and shared community goals. This approach eventually led to the desegregation of Montgomery's buses, proving that controlled, deliberate action can lead to meaningful change even in high-pressure situations.

Exercises

1. **Recognize Escalation Triggers:** Reflect on a recent conflict. What signs indicated escalation? How could you have intervened earlier to redirect the conversation?

2. **Practice De-Escalation Techniques:** Role-play a heated negotiation where one party becomes increasingly rigid. Practice using calming language and reframing to steer the discussion toward resolution.

3. **Analyze a Historical Escalation:** Study a real-world example where escalation spiraled out of control (e.g. a labor strike or international conflict). What could have been done to prevent it?

Key Takeaway

Escalation control is the art of stopping conflicts before they spiral into destruction. By recognizing early signs, interrupting cycles, and redirecting focus, you can preserve relationships and create opportunities for resolution.

Chapter 56: Evolutionary Methods – Adapting to Changing Rules

Why This Matters

The rules of any game — whether in business, negotiations, or life — are rarely static. Evolutionary methods focus on adapting strategies as circumstances evolve, turning change into an opportunity rather than a threat. Inspired by principles from evolutionary biology, these methods are about learning, iterating, and thriving in dynamic environments. As articulated in *The Origin of Wealth* (Beinhocker, 2006), flexibility and adaptability are essential for long-term success.

Mastering evolutionary methods is crucial because rigid strategies fail in the face of unexpected shifts. Whether you're dealing with changing market conditions or unpredictable stakeholders, the ability to adjust your approach ensures resilience and continued progress.

How It Works

Evolutionary methods operate on three principles:

1. **Experimentation:** Test different approaches and learn from successes and failures.

2. **Feedback Loops:** Continuously gather data and refine strategies based on real-world outcomes.

3. **Adaptation:** Embrace flexibility and adjust your plans to align with changing circumstances.

In *Antifragile* (Taleb, 2012), the author emphasizes the value of systems that improve under pressure and change. Evolutionary methods build resilience by turning challenges into opportunities for growth.

Real-Life Example

The Lego Group's turnaround in the early 2000s illustrates the power of evolutionary methods. After facing declining sales and mounting debt, Lego experimented with new products, licensing agreements (like partnerships with *Star Wars* and *Harry Potter*), and digital innovations, including video games and apps. The company also embraced feedback loops by engaging with fans through initiatives like the LEGO Ideas platform, where users submit designs for new products. By continuously adapting to shifts in the toy market and consumer preferences, Lego regained its status as a global leader in the toy industry.

Exercises

1. **Identify Areas for Adaptation:** Think about a current challenge where the "rules" have shifted (e.g., a new technology or competitor). How can you adjust your strategy to stay ahead?

2. **Analyze a Case of Evolution:** Research a company or individual (e.g. a professional athlete) who thrived by adapting to changing circumstances. What lessons can you apply?

3. **Test an Evolutionary Strategy:** Choose a small project and apply an experimental approach. Gather feedback, adjust your methods, and reflect on the outcomes.

Key Takeaway

Evolutionary methods emphasize the importance of adapting strategies to align with changing environments. By experimenting, gathering feedback, and embracing flexibility, you can turn uncertainty into opportunity and thrive in dynamic contexts.

Chapter 57: Hybrid Blueprints – Blending Synergy and Competition

Why This Matters

In complex environments, pure competition or unbridled collaboration rarely leads to optimal outcomes. Hybrid blueprints, which blend elements of synergy and competition, provide a balanced approach that leverages the strengths of both strategies. This dynamic framework is especially effective in industries, organizations, or ecosystems where players must work together while pursuing their interests.

The ability to apply hybrid blueprints is essential because many real-world challenges involve both shared goals and competing priorities. As outlined in *Co-opetition* (Brandenburger & Nalebuff, 1996), combining collaboration and competition enables organizations and individuals to create value while maintaining their edge.

How It Works

Hybrid blueprints thrive on three principles:

1. **Identify Shared Interests:** Find areas where collaboration benefits all parties, such as industry standards or joint ventures.

2. **Maintain Competitive Incentives:** Ensure that competition exists where it drives innovation, efficiency, or differentiation.

3. **Adapt to Context:** Recognize when to shift the balance between cooperation and competition as circumstances evolve.

This approach is particularly effective in markets with overlapping ecosystems. For example, tech companies often collaborate to develop universal platforms (like USB standards) while fiercely competing in their proprietary products.

Real-Life Example

The Airbus and Boeing collaboration on aviation safety standards is a strong example of hybrid blueprints. While these two aerospace giants fiercely compete for market share in commercial aircraft, they also work together through organizations like the International Civil Aviation Organization (ICAO) to establish and improve global safety standards.

By collaborating on safety regulations, the companies ensure passenger trust in air travel, benefiting the entire industry. At the same time, their competitive rivalry drives innovation in fuel efficiency, design, and technology, helping each company maintain its unique edge. This balance of cooperation and competition strengthens the industry as a whole while allowing both Airbus and Boeing to thrive.

Exercises

1. **Map a Hybrid Opportunity:** Identify a situation where you collaborate with competitors (e.g. shared resources, mutual goals). How can you balance cooperation and competition to maximize value?

2. **Analyze a Hybrid Success Story:** Research an example of co-opetition (e.g. vaccine development or tech alliances). What lessons can you learn from their approach?

3. **Simulate a Hybrid Strategy:** In a negotiation scenario, practice collaborating with a competitor on shared goals while maintaining a competitive edge in other areas. Reflect on the dynamics and outcomes.

Key Takeaway

Hybrid blueprints blend synergy and competition to create balanced strategies for complex environments. By identifying shared interests and maintaining competitive incentives, you can achieve innovation, efficiency, and mutual success.

Chapter 58: Liability Diversification – Spreading Bets for Stability

If one revenue stream dips, the others keep us afloat.

Exactly—diversifying protects us from surprises.

ONLINE SALES

SUBSCRIPTIONS

CONSULTING

Why This Matters

Uncertainty is an inherent part of decision-making. Liability diversification involves spreading risks across multiple areas to ensure that failure in one aspect does not lead to complete collapse. This principle is widely used in finance but applies equally to negotiations, business strategies, and personal decision-making. As emphasized in *The Intelligent Investor* (Graham, 1949), diversification acts as a safety net, protecting against volatility and unexpected shocks.

Liability diversification matters because it minimizes the impact of unforeseen events. By avoiding over-reliance on a single strategy, resource, or outcome, you can build resilience and adapt to challenges more effectively. Whether managing a portfolio, leading a project, or navigating personal goals, spreading risks ensures stability and sustainability.

How It Works

Diversification relies on three core principles:

1. **Distribute Risks:** Spread liabilities across multiple options or areas to reduce vulnerability to any single failure.

2. **Balance Exposure:** Ensure that no single liability dominates, maintaining a proportionate allocation of resources.

3. **Monitor Continuously:** Regularly review your diversified approach to ensure it aligns with changing circumstances.

In *Antifragile* (Taleb, 2012), the author highlights the "barbell strategy," a form of diversification where you combine highly conservative and highly aggressive bets to balance safety and opportunity. This approach ensures protection during downturns while still allowing for significant gains.

Real-Life Example

Sony's diversification across multiple industries demonstrates the value of liability diversification. While Sony is best known for its consumer electronics, it has also invested heavily in other areas, including gaming (PlayStation), entertainment (Sony Pictures and Sony Music), and financial services. This diversification strategy allows Sony to remain resilient during market downturns in any one sector. For example, when competition in the electronics market became intense, the company's gaming and entertainment divisions helped stabilize overall revenue.

This approach has enabled Sony to thrive despite challenges in individual business lines, showcasing how spreading risks across diverse industries can ensure long-term stability.

Exercises

1. **Assess Your Diversification:** Identify a project, investment, or strategy you're currently pursuing. Are you overly reliant on a single option? How can you distribute risks more effectively?

2. **Analyze a Case of Failure Due to Lack of Diversification:** Research a business or organization that struggled due to over-reliance on one resource (e.g. Kodak's dependence on film). What lessons can you learn from their experience?

3. **Plan a Barbell Strategy:** In a negotiation or decision-making scenario, create a plan that balances low-risk and high-reward options. Reflect on how this approach improves your overall stability.

Key Takeaway

Liability diversification ensures resilience by spreading risks across multiple areas. By distributing liabilities, balancing exposure, and staying adaptable, you can minimize the impact of unexpected challenges and maintain stability.

Chapter 59: The Cost of Complexity – Simplifying to Stay Ahead

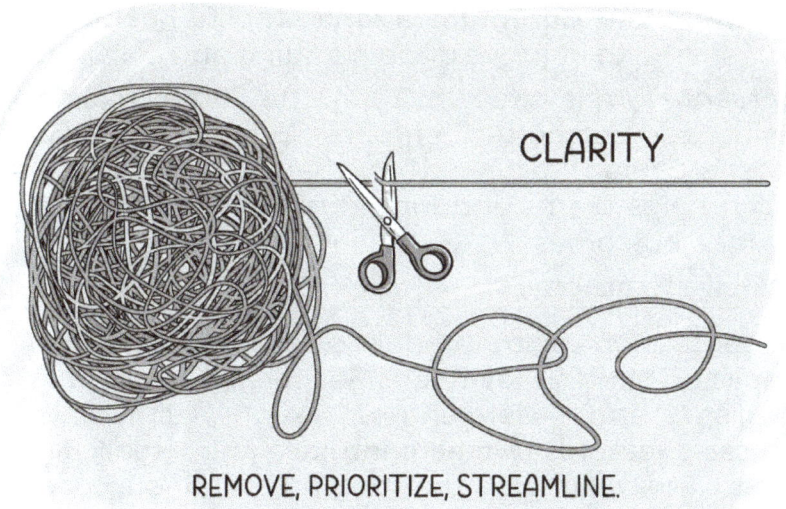

CLARITY

REMOVE, PRIORITIZE, STREAMLINE.

Why This Matters

In an interconnected world, complexity often feels inevitable. However, unchecked complexity can lead to inefficiency, confusion, and missed opportunities. Simplifying processes, decisions, and strategies allows you to focus on what truly matters, enabling better outcomes. As discussed in *The Laws of Simplicity* (Maeda, 2006), simplicity is not about removing important elements but making the complex more manageable and meaningful.

Understanding the cost of complexity is critical because excessive layers—whether in business models, decision-making processes, or negotiations—can obscure goals and reduce effectiveness. Simplification fosters clarity, improves communication, and ensures that resources are used efficiently.

How It Works

Reducing complexity involves three key steps:

1. **Identify Bottlenecks:** Pinpoint areas where excessive layers or unclear processes are creating inefficiencies.
2. **Prioritize Core Elements:** Focus on essential goals and remove unnecessary steps or distractions.
3. **Streamline Communication:** Simplify how information is shared to improve understanding and collaboration.

In *Essentialism* (McKeown, 2014), the author highlights the power of "less but better," emphasizing that simplification is about sharpening focus rather than cutting corners. This approach helps teams and individuals align their efforts with meaningful outcomes.

Real-Life Example

The success of Apple's product design illustrates the power of simplicity. Under Steve Jobs' leadership, Apple prioritized minimalism and user-centric designs, stripping away unnecessary features to create intuitive and visually appealing products. For example, the original iPod succeeded not because it was the most feature-rich device but because it was easy to use, with a simple interface and slogan: "1,000 songs in your pocket." By reducing complexity, Apple revolutionized the tech industry and became a leader in innovation.

In a different context, organizations that simplify decision-making processes also benefit. For instance, Southwest Airlines streamlined its operations by focusing on a single type of aircraft (the Boeing 737), reducing training and maintenance costs. This simplification contributed to the company's reputation for efficiency and profitability in a highly competitive industry.

Exercises

1. **Simplify a Process:** Identify a task or workflow that feels unnecessarily complex. Break it down into its core components and remove steps or features that don't add significant value.

2. **Analyze a Simplification Success Story:** Research a company or product (e.g., Apple or Southwest Airlines) known for successful simplification. What strategies did they use, and what were the outcomes?

3. **Streamline Your Communication:** Practice explaining a complex idea in the simplest terms possible, using no more than three key points. Reflect on how this exercise improves clarity.

Key Takeaway

The cost of complexity can drain resources and obscure goals. By identifying bottlenecks, prioritizing essentials, and streamlining processes, you can simplify effectively, stay focused, and achieve better outcomes.

Chapter 60: Behavioral Insights – Using Psychology to Your Advantage

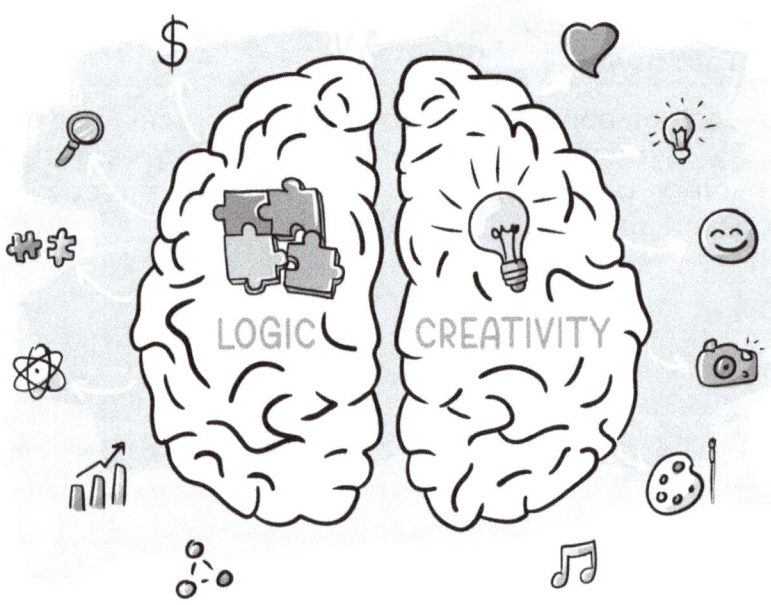

Why This Matters

Human behavior is often driven by unconscious biases, emotions, and heuristics. Behavioral insights involve understanding these psychological drivers to make better decisions and influence others effectively. Concepts from behavioral economics, popularized by Daniel Kahneman's *Thinking, Fast and Slow* (2011) and Richard Thaler's *Nudge* (2008), reveal how subtle shifts in framing or incentives can lead to significant changes in behavior.

Mastering behavioral insights matters because it equips you to navigate and shape complex interactions. Whether you're negotiating, managing a team, or designing policies, leveraging psychological principles helps you align actions with goals, reduce conflict, and foster better outcomes.

How It Works

Behavioral insights rely on understanding three key psychological principles:

1. **Cognitive Biases:** Recognize common biases like anchoring, loss aversion, and confirmation bias to avoid their pitfalls and use them strategically.

2. **Framing Effects:** Present information in ways that highlight desired outcomes. For example, emphasizing gains ("Save 20%") is often more effective than highlighting losses ("Avoid a 20% loss").

3. **Choice Architecture:** Design environments that guide decisions subtly, such as arranging healthy food at eye level in cafeterias to encourage better eating habits.

In *Nudge* (Thaler & Sunstein, 2008), the authors describe how small environmental or contextual changes can "nudge" people toward better choices without restricting their freedom.

Real-Life Example

The Save More Tomorrow (SMarT) program by Thaler and Shlomo Benartzi is a classic application of behavioral insights. This retirement savings plan leverages the principle of default choices and inertia by automatically enrolling employees in savings increases tied to future raises. Since people are more likely to commit to actions that don't require immediate sacrifice, the program significantly increased savings rates among participants.

Exercises

1. **Identify Biases in Action:** Reflect on a recent decision you made. Can you identify any cognitive biases that influenced your choice? How might you overcome or leverage these biases in the future?

2. **Practice Framing Techniques:** Take a message or offer and write two versions: one emphasizing gains and the other losses. Test which version is more persuasive with a colleague or friend.

3. **Design a Choice Environment:** Create a scenario where you design a system to encourage better behavior (e.g. increasing participation in a survey or encouraging recycling). Consider how small changes in presentation or defaults could impact outcomes.

Key Takeaway

Behavioral insights reveal how psychology drives decisions and actions. By understanding cognitive biases, framing effects, and choice architecture, you can navigate complex interactions, influence behavior, and achieve better results.

Part 7: Game Theory in Everyday Life

Game theory isn't confined to boardrooms, negotiations, or international diplomacy. It plays a pivotal role in daily life. This section explores how game theory principles apply to common challenges, from managing relationships and motivating teams to handling risk and uncertainty. You'll learn how to negotiate with irrational players, align incentives for success, and harness concepts like reputation and trust to build long-term advantages. These chapters transform abstract strategies into practical tools you can use to make smarter decisions, build stronger connections, and navigate everyday complexities with confidence.

Chapter 61: Negotiating with Irrational Players – Keeping Calm Under Chaos

Why This Matters

Negotiating with irrational players — those driven by emotion, stubbornness, or erratic behavior — can feel like navigating a storm. Their unpredictability and refusal to follow logical paths make it difficult to reach agreements. However, by staying calm and applying structured strategies, you can manage these interactions effectively. As highlighted in *Getting Past No* (Ury, 1991), maintaining composure and redirecting the energy of chaos can lead even the most challenging discussions toward productive outcomes.

This skill matters because irrational players are a part of life, whether they're colleagues, clients, or family members. Learning how to negotiate with them ensures you can protect your interests while fostering cooperation instead of conflict.

How It Works

Negotiating with irrational players requires a balance of patience, emotional regulation, and strategic redirection. Key steps include:

1. **Acknowledge Their Emotions:** Recognize and validate the emotions driving their behavior, such as anger or frustration, without conceding your position.
2. **Reframe the Conversation:** Shift focus from emotional reactions to shared goals or benefits.
3. **Stay Grounded:** Avoid being drawn into their chaos by maintaining a calm and neutral demeanor.

In *Crucial Conversations* (Patterson et al., 2002), the authors emphasize the importance of creating a safe environment for dialogue. Establishing trust and showing empathy can often defuse irrationality and pave the way for constructive negotiation.

Real-Life Example

A well-known example is Abraham Lincoln's strategy during his presidency. Lincoln was known for dealing with difficult, irrational individuals, including political rivals and wartime generals. Instead of reacting emotionally, he often used humor, empathy, and carefully chosen words to defuse tensions. His ability to stay calm and focus on the broader goals of the Union allowed him to manage conflicts effectively, even under immense pressure.

On a personal level, consider a workplace dispute where a colleague reacts irrationally to constructive feedback. Instead of escalating the conflict, acknowledging their emotions ("I understand this must be frustrating") and redirecting the focus to shared goals ("Let's figure out how we can solve this together") can turn a volatile situation into a collaborative one.

Exercises

1. **Practice Staying Calm:** Think of a recent situation where someone acted irrationally. Reflect on how you reacted and write down strategies you could use to stay calm and composed next time.

2. **Role-Play with a Partner:** Simulate a negotiation where one person acts irrationally. Practice using acknowledgment, reframing, and grounding techniques to guide the conversation back on track.

3. **Study a Historical Example:** Research how a historical leader or negotiator dealt with irrational individuals (e.g., Lincoln, Mandela). What strategies did they use to stay calm and resolve the situation?

Key Takeaway

Negotiating with irrational players requires patience, empathy, and strategic redirection. By staying composed, acknowledging emotions, and focusing on shared goals, you can turn chaotic interactions into opportunities for progress.

Chapter 62: Frictionless Output – Reducing Barriers to Teamwork

Why This Matters

Teamwork is often hindered by unnecessary friction — miscommunication, unclear roles, or conflicting priorities. Frictionless output focuses on reducing these barriers to create smoother collaboration and improved results. As outlined in *The Five Dysfunctions of a Team* (Lencioni, 2002), eliminating friction not only enhances productivity but also strengthens trust and cohesion within teams.

Mastering frictionless output is crucial because teams are the foundation of most successful organizations and projects. Removing obstacles allows each member to contribute their best, fostering innovation and achieving goals more efficiently.

How It Works

Creating frictionless teamwork involves:

1. **Clarify Roles and Goals:** Ensure that everyone understands their responsibilities and how their contributions align with the team's objectives.

2. **Streamline Communication:** Use clear, concise communication to avoid misunderstandings and encourage transparency.

3. **Encourage Collaboration:** Create a culture where team members feel comfortable sharing ideas, asking questions, and providing feedback.

In *Drive* (Pink, 2009), the author highlights how intrinsic motivation — autonomy, mastery, and purpose — thrives in environments with reduced friction, leading to more engaged and effective teams.

Real-Life Example

Pixar Animation Studios provides an excellent example of frictionless teamwork. The company fosters collaboration by creating an open feedback culture, where team members from all levels and departments are encouraged to contribute ideas. This approach eliminates hierarchical barriers and ensures the best ideas rise to the surface, leading to ground-breaking films like *Toy Story* and *Inside Out*.

In a smaller-scale example, a remote team working across time zones can reduce friction by implementing clear communication tools (e.g. Slack, Trello) and establishing regular check-ins to align goals. These practices streamline workflows and minimize misunderstandings, ensuring everyone stays on track.

Exercises

1. **Identify Team Frictions:** Think about a team or group you're part of. List the most common sources of friction and brainstorm ways to address them (e.g. clarifying goals, improving tools).

2. **Analyze a Collaborative Success:** Research an organization or project known for exceptional teamwork (e.g. NASA's Apollo missions). What practices contributed to their success?

3. **Create a Collaboration Plan:** Design a plan for improving teamwork within your own context. Include strategies for clarifying roles, streamlining communication, and encouraging feedback.

Key Takeaway

Frictionless teamwork eliminates barriers that hinder productivity and collaboration. By clarifying roles, improving communication, and fostering a collaborative culture, teams can achieve seamless output and greater success.

Chapter 63: Timing the Market – Knowing When to Act

PERFECT TIMING

Why This Matters

Timing is everything when making decisions, whether in financial markets, negotiations, or everyday choices. Timing the market refers to the strategic act of identifying the optimal moment to take action, based on analysis and anticipation of future trends. While often associated with investing, the principle applies broadly to life and business, where acting too early or too late can result in missed opportunities or increased risks.

Mastering timing matters because the consequences of decisions are rarely uniform over time. Acting with foresight allows you to capitalize on opportunities and avoid costly mistakes, turning the timing itself into a competitive advantage.

How It Works

Timing the market involves three key elements:

1. **Gather Information:** Monitor trends, patterns, and external factors that might influence outcomes. In financial markets, this could mean analyzing historical data or economic indicators.

2. **Anticipate Future Moves:** Use strategic foresight to predict how events may unfold. This involves scenario planning and considering potential risks.

3. **Act Decisively:** Once the optimal window is identified, act quickly and with confidence to maximize returns or benefits.

In *The Little Book That Still Beats the Market* (Greenblatt, 2010), the author emphasizes the importance of understanding long-term trends rather than reacting impulsively. Success often comes from balancing patience with decisive action when the moment is right.

Real-Life Example

Procter & Gamble's launch of Tide Pods illustrates the importance of timing in innovation. By introducing Tide Pods in 2012, P&G capitalized on growing consumer demand for convenience and single-use products. The company's extensive market research revealed a shift in consumer preferences toward simpler and more efficient solutions for household tasks. By waiting until the market was ready for this innovation — when consumers were accustomed to single-serve products like K-Cups — they ensured a successful product launch. Tide Pods quickly became a market leader, driving significant growth for P&G in the laundry detergent category.

Exercises

1. **Evaluate Past Timing:** Reflect on a recent decision where timing was critical. Did you act too early, too late, or at the right moment? What factors influenced your timing?

2. **Practice Trend Analysis:** Choose a market or field (e.g., real estate, technology) and identify current trends. Consider how you might act strategically based on these patterns.

3. **Simulate Timing Scenarios:** Create a hypothetical situation where timing matters, such as launching a product or entering a negotiation. Plan your actions based on different timing windows and reflect on the outcomes.

Key Takeaway

Timing the market is about recognizing and seizing opportunities at the right moment. By gathering information, anticipating future moves, and acting decisively, you can maximize benefits and minimize risks in any decision-making process.

Chapter 64: Repetition and Reputation – Reaching Your Goals Through Consistency

CONSISTENCY

Why This Matters

Consistency is the foundation of mastery, trust, and influence. Repetition builds competence through practice and refinement, while reputation amplifies your credibility and opens doors to opportunities. Together, they create a cycle where consistent actions not only drive personal improvement but also establish how others perceive and trust you. As James Clear explains in *Atomic Habits* (2018), small, repeated behaviors compound into extraordinary outcomes, often surpassing initial expectations.

Reputation and repetition matter because they set the stage for long-term success. Consistent effort allows you to improve incrementally, while a strong reputation attracts collaboration, loyalty, and opportunities that align with your goals. By leveraging these principles, you can make steady progress in any area of life, from building a career to fostering relationships.

How It Works

Achieving success through repetition and reputation involves three critical steps:

1. **Establish Core Habits:** Repetition requires identifying small, repeatable actions that align with your long-term goals. This could involve daily practice, regular check-ins with a team, or maintaining high standards in every project. As highlighted in *The Power of Habit* (Duhigg, 2012), habits simplify the path to improvement by reducing decision fatigue and reinforcing positive behaviors.

2. **Deliver Consistently:** Reputation is built on trust, which grows when people see you deliver reliable results. Whether meeting deadlines, keeping promises, or maintaining professionalism, consistent actions shape how others perceive your dependability. Over time, this builds a reputation that precedes you, opening doors to greater opportunities.

3. **Leverage Momentum:** Repetition creates momentum that builds confidence and expertise. As you improve through practice, your reputation amplifies your reach, leading to a compounding effect where each success reinforces the next.

This cycle of repetition and reputation is not about perfection but persistence. Even small, consistent efforts can lead to transformative outcomes, both in skill development and relationship-building.

Real-Life Example

The legendary career of Serena Williams epitomizes the power of repetition and reputation. Through relentless practice and unwavering focus, Serena refined her skills, becoming one of the most accomplished athletes in history. Her consistency on the tennis court—winning 23 Grand Slam titles—built a reputation that transcends sports. Beyond her athletic achievements, Serena's reputation for discipline and resilience has made her a role model, securing sponsorships, business ventures, and a lasting legacy.

In everyday contexts, repetition and reputation play an equally critical role. Consider a freelancer building their career. By consistently delivering high-quality work on time, they earn the trust of clients, leading to repeat business and glowing referrals. Over time, their reputation as a reliable professional becomes a magnet for opportunities, enabling growth without constant self-promotion.

Exercises

1. **Track a Habit:** Identify a skill or goal you want to improve. Break it into daily or weekly actions, and track your progress for 30 days. Reflect on how repetition strengthens your confidence and results.

2. **Evaluate Your Reputation:** Write down three adjectives you think others associate with you professionally or personally. How do your actions support or detract from this perception? What steps can you take to enhance your reputation?

3. **Analyze a Role Model:** Research someone known for their consistency and strong reputation (e.g. an artist, entrepreneur, or leader). What habits or actions contributed to their success? How can you apply similar strategies in your own journey?

Key Takeaway

Repetition fuels personal growth, while reputation builds trust and influence. By focusing on consistent effort and delivering reliable results, you create a compounding effect that propels you toward long-term success in any endeavor.

Chapter 65: Incentive Alignment – Motivating Others Effectively

ALIGNED INCENTIVES

Why This Matters

Motivating others is one of the most critical challenges in leadership, teamwork, and negotiations. Misaligned incentives can lead to inefficiency, conflict, or outright failure, as individuals prioritize their own goals over the group's objectives. Incentive alignment ensures that everyone's motivations are directed toward a common purpose, creating a win-win dynamic where individual efforts contribute to collective success.

This concept matters because it bridges the gap between intention and action. When incentives are properly aligned, they encourage collaboration, increase productivity, and foster trust. As Dan Pink emphasizes in *Drive* (2009), intrinsic motivators like autonomy, mastery, and purpose are just as important as external rewards in ensuring long-term engagement.

How It Works

Aligning incentives involves three key steps:

1. **Understand Motivations:** Identify what drives each individual—whether it's financial rewards, recognition, autonomy, or personal growth.

2. **Design Fair Rewards:** Create systems where rewards reflect contributions and encourage collaboration. Avoid structures that foster competition within teams when cooperation is needed.

3. **Communicate Shared Goals:** Clearly articulate how individual efforts align with broader organizational or team objectives.

In *Thinking, Fast and Slow* (Kahneman, 2011), the author highlights how cognitive biases can lead to misaligned incentives. Leaders must recognize these biases to design frameworks that truly motivate and align stakeholders effectively.

Real-Life Example

The success of Wikipedia showcases the power of aligned incentives. Unlike traditional organizations, Wikipedia relies on thousands of volunteers to create and maintain its content. The platform's incentive structure is intrinsic rather than financial — contributors are motivated by the opportunity to share knowledge, gain recognition within the community, and be part of a larger mission to make information accessible to everyone. This alignment of individual passions with Wikipedia's overarching goal has allowed it to thrive as the world's largest online encyclopedia.

In professional contexts, aligned incentives are critical in commission-based sales teams. For example, companies that implement team-based bonuses rather than individual commissions encourage collaboration and discourage unhealthy competition. This alignment fosters a supportive environment where team members work together to achieve collective success.

Exercises

1. **Identify Incentives:** Choose a team or project you're part of and list the incentives currently in place. Are they aligned with the group's goals, or do they create unintended conflicts?

2. **Redesign a System:** Take a flawed incentive structure (real or hypothetical) and redesign it to encourage collaboration and alignment. Reflect on how these changes improve outcomes.

3. **Analyze a Success Story:** Research an organization or initiative (e.g. Wikipedia) that successfully uses aligned incentives. What lessons can you apply to your own context?

Key Takeaway

Aligned incentives motivate individuals to work toward shared goals while minimizing conflicts. By understanding motivations, designing fair rewards, and communicating a clear purpose, you can foster collaboration and drive collective success.

Chapter 66: Loss Aversion – Turning Fear into Opportunity

Why This Matters

Humans are wired to fear losses more than they value equivalent gains — a phenomenon known as loss aversion. This psychological bias, first studied by Daniel Kahneman and Amos Tversky in *Prospect Theory* (1979), explains why people often avoid risks even when the potential rewards outweigh the costs. While loss aversion can lead to cautious behavior, understanding and reframing it allows you to make better decisions and turn fear into opportunity.

Loss aversion matters because it affects decision-making in every aspect of life, from investing and negotiations to personal relationships. Recognizing this bias helps you manage fear more effectively and make rational choices that align with long-term goals.

How It Works

Turning loss aversion into an advantage involves:

1. **Recognize the Bias:** Be aware of situations where fear of loss is driving your decisions. Ask yourself whether the perceived risk is greater than the actual likelihood of loss.

2. **Reframe the Decision:** Focus on the potential gains rather than the losses. For example, instead of fearing a failed investment, consider the knowledge and experience gained from trying.

3. **Take Calculated Risks:** Mitigate losses through diversification, preparation, or setting clear limits while still pursuing opportunities.

In *The Art of Thinking Clearly* (Dobelli, 2013), the author emphasizes that managing loss aversion requires shifting your perspective and seeing setbacks as learning experiences rather than permanent failures.

Real-Life Example

Elon Musk's investment in SpaceX provides an excellent example of overcoming loss aversion. In 2008, after three failed rocket launches, Musk faced financial ruin and immense public scrutiny. Instead of giving up, Musk reframed the potential losses as stepping stones toward eventual success. He took the calculated risk of funding one final launch with nearly all his remaining resources. That fourth launch succeeded, earning NASA contracts that secured SpaceX's future and revolutionized space travel. Musk's ability to embrace potential losses and focus on the long-term vision turned a near-catastrophe into ground-breaking innovation.

Exercises

1. **Identify a Fear of Loss:** Reflect on a recent decision where fear of loss influenced your actions. How could you have reframed the situation to focus on the potential gains?

2. **Simulate a Negotiation:** Practice a negotiation scenario where one party fears rejection or failure. Work on reframing their perspective to emphasize opportunities instead of risks.

3. **Analyze a Risk-Taker's Story:** Research a successful entrepreneur or leader who took significant risks despite potential losses. What mindset shifts allowed them to overcome loss aversion?

Key Takeaway

Loss aversion is a natural bias, but it doesn't have to hold you back. By recognizing fear-driven decisions, reframing risks as opportunities, and taking calculated actions, you can transform hesitation into progress.

Chapter 67: Prospect Theory – Seeing Challenges the Right Way

Why This Matters

The way challenges are framed profoundly impacts how people respond to them. Prospect theory, introduced by Daniel Kahneman and Amos Tversky, demonstrates that individuals don't evaluate gains and losses objectively. Instead, they make decisions based on perceived value relative to a reference point, often overweighing losses compared to equivalent gains. Understanding this principle allows you to approach challenges strategically and influence how others perceive risks and opportunities.

Prospect theory matters because it helps you navigate decision-making with greater clarity. By recognizing how framing affects behavior, you can make smarter choices, reduce emotional biases, and present challenges in ways that inspire confidence and action.

How It Works

Prospect theory operates on three key principles:

1. **Loss Aversion:** People feel the pain of losses more acutely than the pleasure of equivalent gains. For example, losing $100 feels worse than the joy of winning $100.

2. **Reference Points:** Decisions are influenced by how outcomes are framed relative to a baseline. What feels like a gain in one context might feel like a loss in another.

3. **Framing Effects:** The same situation can evoke different reactions depending on whether it's presented as a potential gain or a potential loss.

In *Thinking, Fast and Slow* (Kahneman, 2011), the author explains that understanding these biases is essential for overcoming them and making more rational decisions.

Real-Life Example

The London congestion charge is a real-world application of prospect theory. Introduced in 2003, the policy was framed as a loss: drivers entering central London during peak hours would pay a daily charge. This framing played on loss aversion, discouraging unnecessary trips and reducing congestion. The policy successfully shifted behavior by leveraging psychological biases, demonstrating how framing can shape outcomes effectively.

On a personal level, consider someone trying to save money. Framing savings as "losing" discretionary spending often feels restrictive. However, reframing the same action as "gaining financial freedom" encourages a more positive perspective, increasing motivation to save.

Exercises

1. **Reframe a Challenge:** Think of a current problem you're facing. How can you reframe it as an opportunity or potential gain instead of focusing on what might be lost?

2. **Analyze a Decision:** Reflect on a past decision where loss aversion influenced your choice. How might a different framing have led to a better outcome?

3. **Simulate Framing Effects:** Present a hypothetical scenario to a friend or colleague in two ways: one emphasizing potential losses and the other potential gains. Observe how the framing changes their response.

Key Takeaway

Prospect theory reveals how perceptions of gains and losses shape decision-making. By reframing challenges as opportunities and recognizing biases, you can approach decisions with greater clarity and inspire action in others.

Chapter 68: The Role of Luck – Managing the Uncontrollable

Why This Matters

Luck plays a larger role in success and failure than most people acknowledge. While hard work, preparation, and skill are critical, luck often serves as the tipping point in achieving extraordinary outcomes. Managing the uncontrollable doesn't mean eliminating luck but rather positioning yourself to maximize its benefits while mitigating its downsides. As Nassim Taleb explores in *Fooled by Randomness* (2001), understanding luck's role helps you make decisions grounded in reality rather than illusion.

This concept matters because failing to recognize the role of luck can lead to overconfidence in success or undue blame for failure. By understanding luck's influence, you can make more informed decisions and prepare for uncertainty with greater resilience.

How It Works

Managing luck involves three strategies:

1. **Create Opportunities:** Increase your exposure to luck by taking calculated risks, networking, and staying open to new experiences.

2. **Focus on Controllables:** While luck can't be controlled, preparation, skill, and effort improve the chances of favorable outcomes.

3. **Learn from Outcomes:** Distinguish between decisions influenced by skill versus luck, using reflection to refine your approach.

In *The Success Equation* (Mauboussin, 2012), the author emphasizes how understanding the balance between skill and luck helps individuals and organizations navigate uncertainty effectively.

Real-Life Example

The rise of Google illustrates the interplay of skill and luck. While Google's founders, Larry Page and Sergey Brin, developed a superior search engine, their success was bolstered by fortunate timing. The internet was rapidly expanding, and their product launched at a moment when users desperately needed better search tools. Additionally, their initial funding came from a chance meeting with an investor. While their skill was undeniable, luck played a key role in their meteoric rise.

On a personal level, consider a job opportunity gained through networking. While hard work and qualifications are critical, a chance meeting at the right time can often open unexpected doors. Recognizing the role of luck in such scenarios helps you appreciate opportunities and prepare for them when they arise.

Exercises

1. **Reflect on a Lucky Break:** Think of a time when luck played a role in your success. What factors made you ready to capitalize on that opportunity?

2. **Increase Your Exposure to Luck:** Identify one area in your life where you can take more calculated risks or meet new people. Record how these efforts create new opportunities over time.

3. **Analyze Skill vs. Luck:** Choose a well-known success story (e.g. a company, athlete, or artist). Break down how much of their success can be attributed to skill versus luck.

Key Takeaway

Luck is an uncontrollable yet powerful force in success. By creating opportunities, focusing on preparation, and recognizing luck's influence, you can position yourself to capitalize on favorable circumstances and navigate uncertainty effectively.

Chapter 69: Trust Building – Creating Long-Term Alliances

Why This Matters

Trust is the cornerstone of any meaningful relationship, whether in business, negotiations, or personal life. Building trust ensures cooperation, reduces conflict, and lays the foundation for long-term alliances. As Stephen M.R. Covey explains in *The Speed of Trust* (2006), trust accelerates progress and improves efficiency by eliminating the need for constant oversight and doubt.

Mastering trust-building is essential because trust isn't a static asset — it requires deliberate actions and consistent effort. By fostering reliability, honesty, and transparency, you create relationships that withstand challenges and grow stronger over time.

How It Works

Building trust involves three critical principles:

1. **Consistency:** Deliver on promises and demonstrate reliability over time. People trust actions more than words.

2. **Transparency:** Communicate openly and honestly, especially in difficult situations. Avoid hidden agendas or manipulation.

3. **Empathy:** Show genuine concern for others' needs and perspectives, fostering mutual respect and understanding.

In *Never Split the Difference* (Voss, 2016), the author highlights how trust is built in negotiations by listening actively, demonstrating empathy, and finding ways to create shared value. These small but deliberate actions strengthen bonds, even in high-stakes scenarios.

Real-Life Example

The partnership between Starbucks and PepsiCo exemplifies trust building in a long-term alliance. In the 1990s, Starbucks wanted to expand its ready-to-drink coffee products but lacked the distribution capabilities to reach global markets. PepsiCo, with its extensive distribution network, became a strategic partner. Over time, the two companies built trust through consistent communication, shared objectives, and successful product launches like bottled Frappuccinos. This alliance continues to thrive, demonstrating how mutual trust can lead to enduring collaboration and sustained growth for both parties.

Exercises

1. **Evaluate Your Trustworthiness:** Reflect on a relationship where trust is critical. Are your actions consistent, transparent, and empathetic? Identify one area to improve.

2. **Analyze a Trust-Building Partnership:** Research a successful business alliance. What specific actions built and maintained trust between the parties?

3. **Practice Active Listening:** In your next conversation, focus entirely on understanding the other person's perspective. Reflect on how this action strengthens trust in the relationship.

Key Takeaway

Trust-building requires consistency, transparency, and empathy. By fostering these qualities, you can create strong, enduring alliances that withstand challenges and drive mutual success.

Chapter 70: The Domino Effect – Anticipating Chain Reactions

Why This Matters

Every decision humans make creates ripples that extend far beyond the immediate action. The domino effect refers to this chain reaction, where one event sets off a series of consequences, often in unexpected ways. Understanding this dynamic allows you to anticipate outcomes, plan for contingencies, and make choices with greater foresight.

Mastering the domino effect is crucial because it helps you avoid unintended consequences while leveraging positive momentum. As Peter Senge explains in *The Fifth Discipline* (1990), systems thinking—the ability to see connections and anticipate ripple effects — is key to long-term success in complex environments.

How It Works

Anticipating the domino effect involves three steps:

1. **Map the System:** Visualize how a single decision will impact related areas, identifying direct and indirect consequences.

2. **Plan for Contingencies:** Consider how you can mitigate negative effects or amplify positive ones.

3. **Monitor the Impact:** Continuously assess how initial actions are influencing the system, and adjust your strategy accordingly.

In *Thinking in Systems* (Meadows, 2008), the author emphasizes the importance of feedback loops—understanding how actions influence outcomes over time — to navigate complex systems effectively.

Real-Life Example

The Marshall Plan after World War II demonstrates the power of the domino effect in international policy. By investing in the economic recovery of European nations, the United States not only helped rebuild war-torn economies but also stabilized global markets, strengthened alliances, and curtailed the spread of communism. This chain reaction of positive outcomes stemmed from a single, well-considered initiative.

In everyday life, consider the domino effect of small daily habits. For example, developing a morning routine that includes exercise and planning can set the tone for a productive day, which leads to achieving long-term goals. These small, consistent actions create a cascading impact on overall success.

Exercises

1. **Trace a Domino Effect:** Reflect on a recent decision you made. Map out the immediate and longer-term consequences that resulted. What lessons can you apply to future decisions?

2. **Plan for Ripple Effects:** Choose a pending decision and brainstorm possible outcomes. Identify both positive and negative chain reactions, and develop strategies to amplify benefits or mitigate risks.

3. **Analyze a Historic Chain Reaction:** Research an event with significant ripple effects (e.g. the Marshall Plan). How did one decision create broader consequences?

Key Takeaway

The domino effect highlights how one decision sets off a series of outcomes. By mapping systems, planning contingencies, and monitoring impacts, you can anticipate ripple effects and make choices that lead to positive, lasting results.

Part 8: Advanced Game Theory Applications

As you deepen your understanding of game theory, it's time to explore strategies that demand a higher level of precision and foresight. This section delves into advanced applications, from adopting a master player's mindset to controlling the flow of information, sending powerful signals, and managing competition effectively. These chapters focus on techniques that sharpen decision-making, prevent costly missteps, and ensure you maintain an edge in complex scenarios. Whether you're navigating high-stakes negotiations or competing in crowded markets, these strategies equip you to stay ahead, adapt intelligently, and maximize long-term success.

Chapter 71: The Superior Mindset – Act Like a Master Player

Why This Matters

Mastering the game requires more than just playing it—it demands thinking like the best players. The superior mindset is about understanding the broader landscape, anticipating moves several steps ahead, and approaching every decision with a blend of strategy, patience, and confidence. It's the difference between reactive and proactive decision-making.

This mindset matters because success in high-stakes situations often depends on your ability to stay calm under pressure, think critically, and act decisively. Adopting a master player's perspective transforms challenges into opportunities and ensures you're always prepared for what comes next.

How It Works

Developing the superior mindset involves three critical elements:

1. **Think Multiple Moves Ahead:** Like a chess master, visualize the potential outcomes of your decisions and how they interact with others' moves.
2. **Focus on the Long Game:** Prioritize strategies that maximize long-term benefits over short-term gains.
3. **Stay Adaptable:** Be prepared to adjust your approach based on changing dynamics or unforeseen circumstances.

In *The Art of Strategy* (Dixit & Nalebuff, 2008), the authors emphasize that thinking strategically involves placing yourself in others' shoes to predict their moves while simultaneously advancing your own goals.

Real-Life Example

Sara Blakely's strategy for building Spanx into a global brand exemplifies the superior mindset. Blakely, the company's founder, approached the shapewear market with a long-term vision to innovate and dominate an underserved niche. Instead of rushing into production without validation, she meticulously tested her prototypes, patented her ideas, and secured partnerships with major retailers like Neiman Marcus. Blakely also focused on branding, turning Spanx into a lifestyle symbol rather than just a product. Her ability to see beyond immediate sales and invest in sustainable growth and customer loyalty transformed Spanx into a billion-dollar company.

Exercises

1. **Visualize the Gameboard:** Choose a current challenge and map out all the possible moves and outcomes. Consider how your decisions will influence others and how you'll respond to their moves.
2. **Play the Long Game:** Reflect on a decision you've made recently. Did it prioritize long-term benefits or short-term gains? How might you approach similar decisions differently in the future?

3. **Study a Master Player:** Research a successful leader or strategist. What actions or mindsets contributed to their success? How can you apply similar strategies?

Key Takeaway

The superior mindset transforms reactive decision-making into proactive strategy. By thinking ahead, focusing on the long game, and staying adaptable, you position yourself to master any challenge.

Chapter 72: The Role of Information – Controlling the Flow for Victory

Why This Matters

In negotiations, leadership, or problem-solving, information is a currency that can be spent wisely or squandered recklessly. Knowing how to control the flow of information — what to reveal, what to withhold, and when to share — can make the difference between success and failure. Properly managing the timing and volume of information allows you to shape perceptions, influence decisions, and protect your leverage.

This concept matters because overloading others with unnecessary details can create confusion, while withholding critical information at the wrong time can breed mistrust. As explored in *Influence: The Psychology of Persuasion* (Cialdini, 1984), the way information is presented greatly impacts how it is perceived and acted upon, making control of the flow a critical skill in strategic interactions.

How It Works

Mastering the flow of information involves three core strategies:

1. **Curate What Matters:** Identify the most relevant and impactful information for the situation. Avoid revealing unnecessary details that could dilute your message or provide leverage to others.

2. **Control Timing:** Share information when it serves your purpose, such as building trust or strengthening your position.

3. **Frame the Narrative:** Present information in a way that emphasizes your desired perspective, steering the conversation toward your goals.

In *Thinking, Fast and Slow* (Kahneman, 2011), the author highlights how people are influenced by the way information is framed. Strategic framing ensures that what you reveal works in your favor.

Real-Life Example

J.K. Rowling's release of the Harry Potter series demonstrates masterful control of information flow. Rowling maintained strict secrecy about key plot details, building suspense and anticipation among readers. She also strategically revealed hints and teasers during interviews, keeping fans engaged between book releases. This careful management of information not only amplified the series' popularity but also turned every release into a cultural event.

On a personal level, consider how control of information can influence negotiations. For example, during a salary negotiation, a candidate who selectively shares their qualifications and achievements while withholding competing offers until later stages can maintain leverage and increase their chances of securing a better deal.

Exercises

1. **Analyze an Information Flow:** Reflect on a recent situation where the way information was shared influenced the outcome. What worked well, and what could have been handled differently?

2. **Practice Framing Information:** Take a piece of data or news and write two ways to present it—one that highlights positive outcomes and another that emphasizes risks. Observe how the framing changes perceptions.

3. **Plan Your Narrative:** Choose a goal you're working toward (e.g., a presentation or pitch). Decide what key information to share, what to withhold, and the timing for maximum impact.

Key Takeaway

Controlling the flow of information allows you to shape outcomes strategically. By curating what you share, timing it effectively, and framing it persuasively, you can maintain leverage and steer conversations toward success.

Chapter 73: Credible Threats – Using Authority Without Acting

Credible Threat

Why This Matters

A threat loses its value if it's empty or unbelievable. Credible threats are powerful tools in negotiations and leadership because they force others to reconsider their actions without requiring you to follow through. When used effectively, they minimize conflict and maximize influence. However, issuing threats recklessly can erode trust and harm your credibility.

This concept is vital because it allows you to assert authority while maintaining control and reducing unnecessary risks. As highlighted in *Games People Play* (Berne, 1964), the effectiveness of a threat lies not in its delivery but in its perceived plausibility and the stakes it creates.

How It Works

The success of a credible threat depends on three principles:

1. **Build a Reputation for Follow-Through:** People must believe that you are willing and able to carry out your threat if necessary.

2. **Be Clear and Specific:** Clearly communicate what the consequences of inaction or resistance will be, leaving no room for ambiguity.

3. **Use Threats Sparingly:** Overuse or empty threats can harm your credibility and undermine future influence.

Real-Life Example

The Justice Department's antitrust investigation into AT&T and Time Warner's merger in 2017 is a prime example of a credible threat. The government publicly announced that it was prepared to block the merger unless specific conditions were met. Although the case went to court, the announcement alone sent a strong signal that antitrust scrutiny was serious, forcing other companies considering mergers to tread carefully. This credible threat influenced corporate behavior industry-wide without requiring immediate action on every potential case.

In personal contexts, a credible threat might involve a landlord warning of eviction for late rent payments. While the landlord doesn't necessarily want to evict a tenant, the threat—if backed by a history of enforcing such policies — can compel compliance and resolve the issue without escalation.

Exercises

1. **Evaluate a Threat:** Reflect on a time when you issued or faced a threat. Was it credible? How did it influence the outcome? What could have been improved?

2. **Craft a Credible Threat:** Design a mock negotiation scenario where you need to issue a credible threat. Focus on making it specific, believable, and proportional to the situation.

3. **Analyze a Case Study:** Research an example of a credible threat in business or diplomacy (e.g., the AT&T antitrust case). What made the threat effective, and how did it shape outcomes?

Key Takeaway

Credible threats are about influence, not force. By building a reputation for follow-through, communicating clearly, and using threats sparingly, you can assert authority and shape decisions without unnecessary conflict.

Chapter 74: Counterfactual Reasoning – What If and What Next?

Why This Matters

Counterfactual reasoning is the process of considering "what could have been" or "what might be" to improve decision-making and strategy. By analyzing alternate outcomes and potential futures, you can gain critical insights into missed opportunities, plan for contingencies, and refine your approach. This mental exercise allows you to identify mistakes, anticipate challenges, and make smarter, more adaptable choices.

This skill matters because humans are prone to focusing solely on the present or past without adequately preparing for future scenarios. By asking "what if" and "what next," you can broaden your perspective and avoid repeating errors. As explored in *Black Box Thinking* (Syed, 2015), reflecting on hypothetical scenarios often reveals the root causes of failure and opportunities for growth.

How It Works

Counterfactual reasoning operates in two directions:

1. **What If (Backward Thinking):** Analyze past decisions by imagining alternate outcomes. For example, "What if I had acted sooner?" or "What if we had chosen a different strategy?" This retrospective lens helps you identify lessons from past actions.

2. **What Next (Forward Thinking):** Plan for potential futures by considering different paths and their consequences. For instance, "What happens if we launch this product now versus six months later?" Forward-thinking enables strategic preparation for multiple scenarios.

By combining these approaches, you can make decisions with greater clarity and confidence, avoiding past pitfalls while seizing future opportunities.

Real-Life Example

The Titanic disaster in 1912 offers a powerful case of counterfactual reasoning. Following the tragedy, investigators and engineers analyzed the series of decisions that led to the ship's sinking, asking critical "what if" questions. For example, "What if there had been more lifeboats?" or "What if the captain had slowed down in icy waters?" This backward analysis led to sweeping changes in maritime safety regulations, such as mandatory lifeboat requirements and improved iceberg monitoring.

In modern contexts, counterfactual reasoning is widely used in risk management. For instance, businesses often perform scenario analyses to ask "what next" when planning expansions or new product launches, preparing contingency plans for different market conditions.

Exercises

1. **Reflect on a "What If" Scenario:** Think of a decision you regret or a project that didn't succeed. Ask "what if" questions to identify alternate actions you could have taken and what you learned.

2. **Plan a "What Next" Exercise:** Identify a decision you're facing now. Consider at least three possible future outcomes and develop strategies for each.

3. **Analyze a Historical Event:** Choose a historical success or failure (e.g. a major innovation). Explore how "what if" and "what next" questions might have altered the outcome.

Key Takeaway

Counterfactual reasoning sharpens decision-making by examining past outcomes and anticipating future possibilities. By asking "what if" and "what next," you can learn from mistakes, plan for uncertainties, and make smarter, more resilient choices.

Chapter 75: Signaling Power – Sending the Right Messages

I volunteered to lead that high-visibility project—just in time for promotion reviews.

Smart. That sends a clear signal you're ready for leadership.

Why This Matters

In both personal and professional interactions, the signals you send—intentionally or unintentionally—shape how others perceive your intentions, capabilities, and reliability. Signaling power refers to using deliberate cues, messages, or actions to convey confidence, authority, or trustworthiness. When done effectively, signaling can reduce uncertainty, establish credibility, and influence decision-making.

This concept matters because in a world full of noise, people often rely on signals to make quick judgments. As explored in *The Signal and the Noise* (Silver, 2012), separating meaningful signals from irrelevant noise is critical for navigating complex environments and influencing others effectively.

How It Works

Effective signaling involves three core principles:

1. **Clarity:** Ensure that your signal is easily understood by your audience. Ambiguity can dilute its impact.
2. **Authenticity:** Signals must align with your actions and capabilities. Misaligned signals can damage trust and credibility.
3. **Relevance:** Tailor your signal to the specific audience and context. The right message at the wrong time can backfire.

In negotiations, for example, confidence can be signaled through body language, tone, or the strategic release of information. A well-timed signal can establish authority or reassure others, shaping outcomes in your favor.

Real-Life Example

Toyota's commitment to hybrid technology serves as a strong example of signaling power. When Toyota introduced the Prius in the late 1990s, it wasn't just a product launch—it was a signal to consumers and competitors that the company was leading the shift toward environmentally friendly vehicles. By investing heavily in hybrid technology and prominently marketing the Prius, Toyota established itself as an innovator in sustainable transportation, influencing market trends and setting itself apart from competitors.

On a smaller scale, consider how job candidates signal competence during interviews. A well-prepared portfolio, professional demeanor, and specific examples of past achievements send clear signals of capability and reliability, building confidence in their suitability for the role.

Exercises

1. **Identify Your Signals:** Reflect on how your actions, communication, or presentation signal your intentions or capabilities. Are they aligned with your goals?
2. **Analyze a Signal in Action:** Research a company or individual known for their effective signaling (e.g. Toyota with the Prius). What specific signals did they send, and how were they received?

3. **Practice Sending Signals:** In your next interaction—whether a meeting, pitch, or presentation—deliberately send a signal that aligns with your desired outcome. Reflect on its effectiveness.

Key Takeaway

Signaling power is about shaping perceptions through deliberate messages and cues. By sending clear, authentic, and relevant signals, you can establish authority, build trust, and influence outcomes effectively.

Chapter 76: Competitive Positioning – Standing Out in Crowded Markets

Why This Matters

In crowded markets, blending in is a recipe for irrelevance. Competitive positioning is the art of distinguishing yourself, your product, or your organization in a way that captures attention and creates lasting value. By identifying what makes you unique and communicating that effectively, you carve out a space that others cannot easily occupy.

This concept is vital because markets are saturated with options, and decision-makers often face overwhelming choices. As Michael Porter explains in *Competitive Strategy* (1980), companies must decide whether to lead on cost, differentiation, or focus —trying to do it all typically results in mediocrity. Strategic positioning ensures you play to your strengths and maximize your competitive edge.

How It Works

Competitive positioning relies on three key principles:

1. **Identify Your Unique Value:** Determine what sets you apart — this could be quality, cost efficiency, innovation, or emotional appeal.

2. **Know Your Audience:** Tailor your positioning to meet the specific needs and desires of your target market.

3. **Communicate Consistently:** Reinforce your unique value proposition (UVP) through branding, messaging, and actions, ensuring it's memorable and believable.

In *Purple Cow* (Godin, 2003), the author emphasizes that being remarkable — a "purple cow" in a field of ordinary ones — ensures that you stand out and capture attention in even the most competitive spaces.

Real-Life Example

Dyson's entry into the vacuum cleaner market is a masterclass in competitive positioning. When James Dyson launched his bagless vacuum cleaners, he didn't just compete on performance — he framed Dyson vacuums as innovative, sleek, and technologically superior. By focusing on a clear UVP (no loss of suction) and consistent branding, Dyson captured a premium segment of the market despite being priced higher than competitors. His ability to position Dyson products as the must-have choice for tech-savvy, design-conscious consumers propelled the company to global success.

On a smaller scale, competitive positioning can be seen in personal branding. For example, a freelance graphic designer who specializes in eco-friendly packaging design can position themselves as the go-to expert for sustainable brands. By focusing on this niche, they stand out in a sea of generalists.

Exercises

1. **Define Your Unique Selling Points:** Write down three things that make you, your product, or your organization unique. How can you communicate these more effectively to your audience?

2. **Analyze a Successful Brand:** Study a company like Dyson or Tesla (without repeating examples). What positioning strategy did they use, and how did it set them apart?

3. **Test Your Positioning:** Create a short pitch or description of your unique value proposition. Share it with a colleague or friend and get feedback on how clear and compelling it is.

Key Takeaway

Competitive positioning ensures you stand out in crowded markets. By identifying your unique value, knowing your audience, and communicating consistently, you create differentiation that drives success.

Chapter 77: Entry Deterrence – Keeping Rivals Out of Your Territory

Why This Matters

In competitive environments, preventing rivals from entering your territory is often as important as thriving within it. Entry deterrence involves creating barriers that make it difficult, costly, or unappealing for competitors to challenge your position. By securing your market, you protect profits, maintain leadership, and focus on growth without constant disruption.

This concept is crucial because unchecked competition can erode market share, reduce margins, and increase instability. As explored in *The Innovator's Dilemma* (Christensen, 1997), companies that fail to defend their territory often find themselves outflanked by disruptive challengers.

How It Works

Effective entry deterrence involves three strategies:

1. **Erect Barriers:** Build high start-up costs, patents, brand loyalty, or regulatory advantages that make entry unattractive.

2. **Signal Dominance:** Demonstrate your capability and willingness to compete aggressively if challenged, discouraging rivals from entering.

3. **Innovate Continuously:** Stay ahead of competitors by introducing new products, features, or services that raise the bar for market entry.

In *Co-opetition* (Brandenburger & Nalebuff, 1996), the authors emphasize that entry deterrence isn't about destroying competition—it's about securing your position while leaving room for partnerships and mutual benefits when possible.

Real-Life Example

Intel's dominance in the microprocessor market highlights effective entry deterrence. Intel leveraged its massive investments in research and development (R&D) to consistently deliver cutting-edge processors, setting a high bar for competitors. It also used its market influence to establish industry standards that heavily favored its products, making it difficult for new entrants to compete on performance or compatibility. Additionally, Intel maintained strong relationships with hardware manufacturers, ensuring its processors were widely adopted. This combination of innovation, partnerships, and strategic influence kept rivals at bay for decades.

On a smaller scale, entry deterrence can be seen in a local boutique that creates exclusive partnerships with suppliers to ensure unique, high-quality products that competitors cannot easily replicate. This approach not only secures the boutique's market position but also builds customer loyalty.

Exercises

1. **Identify Barriers:** Think about your market or industry. What barriers currently exist to protect your position, and how can you strengthen them?

2. **Analyze a Dominant Player:** Study a company like Intel or another leader in your industry. What entry deterrence strategies have they used, and how effective have they been?

3. **Design a Deterrence Plan:** Imagine a competitor is entering your market. Develop a strategy to deter them, focusing on barriers, signaling, and innovation.

Key Takeaway

Entry deterrence secures your territory by discouraging competitors from entering. By building barriers, signaling dominance, and innovating continuously, you can maintain leadership and focus on long-term growth.

Chapter 78: Managing Missteps – Learning from Failures

Why This Matters

Failures are inevitable, but how you respond to them determines your long-term success. Managing missteps is about turning setbacks into opportunities for growth. By analyzing what went wrong, addressing weaknesses, and applying lessons learned, you can emerge stronger and more resilient. As discussed in *Failing Forward* (Maxwell, 2007), failure is not the opposite of success — it's part of the journey.

This mindset matters because fear of failure often leads to risk aversion, missed opportunities, and stagnation. Embracing mistakes as learning tools allows you to innovate, adapt, and achieve lasting progress.

How It Works

Managing missteps effectively involves three steps:

1. **Reflect:** Take time to analyze the root cause of the failure. What assumptions or actions led to the misstep? Avoid placing blame and focus on understanding the situation objectively.

2. **Adapt:** Develop strategies to address the weaknesses or gaps that caused the failure. This might involve new training, processes, or tools.

3. **Implement Change:** Apply the lessons learned in future decisions, ensuring that past mistakes lead to smarter choices and better outcomes.

In *The Lean Startup* (Ries, 2011), the concept of "build, measure, learn" highlights the value of iterative improvement. Every failure provides valuable data to refine your approach and move closer to success.

Real-Life Example

NASA's lessons from the Challenger disaster exemplify how missteps can lead to transformative change. After the space shuttle Challenger tragically exploded in 1986, NASA conducted an extensive investigation to understand the root causes. The findings revealed issues in organizational communication and decision-making processes. In response, NASA implemented significant reforms, including stricter safety protocols and more transparent communication structures. These changes not only improved future missions but also restored trust in the organization.

On a personal level, consider an entrepreneur whose initial business venture fails due to poor market research. By reflecting on their mistake, they might identify the need to better understand customer needs, leading to a more successful second attempt.

Exercises

1. **Conduct a Failure Audit:** Reflect on a recent failure. What went wrong, and why? What specific lessons can you apply to avoid repeating the same mistakes?

2. **Develop a Resilience Plan:** Create a plan for handling future failures. Include steps for reflection, adaptation, and implementation of changes.

3. **Study a Recovery Story:** Research a company or individual who bounced back from failure (e.g., NASA after Challenger). What actions did they take, and how did they turn their misstep into an advantage?

Key Takeaway

Failure is not the end — it's a step toward improvement. By reflecting on missteps, adapting your approach, and applying lessons learned, you can transform setbacks into stepping stones to success.

Chapter 79: Maximizing Utility – Balancing Functionality and Fairness

Why This Matters

Achieving the best possible outcome often involves trade-offs. Maximizing utility is about balancing functionality (efficiency, practicality) with fairness (equity, inclusiveness). This approach ensures that decisions are both effective and just, fostering sustainable outcomes and trust among stakeholders.

This principle matters because decisions skewed too far toward functionality risk alienating key stakeholders, while prioritizing fairness excessively may hinder productivity. Striking a balance is essential for creating solutions that are both efficient and inclusive, particularly in high-stakes negotiations, leadership, or policy-making.

How It Works

Maximizing utility involves three essential steps:

1. **Assess Stakeholder Needs:** Identify the goals, concerns, and expectations of all parties involved to understand where functionality and fairness align or conflict.
2. **Evaluate Trade-Offs:** Quantify the impacts of prioritizing one dimension (efficiency or equity) over the other. What gains or losses occur in each scenario?
3. **Craft Balanced Solutions:** Design outcomes that optimize practical results while maintaining fairness, ensuring that all parties feel valued and engaged.

In *Thinking Strategically* (Dixit & Nalebuff, 1993), the authors discuss how strategic decision-making often involves considering utility—both in terms of tangible gains and the perceptions of fairness by those affected.

Real-Life Example

The redesign of the public transportation system in Curitiba, Brazil serves as a strong example of maximizing utility. In the 1970s, the city faced rapid population growth and increasing traffic congestion. City planners prioritized efficiency by creating the Bus Rapid Transit (BRT) system, which allowed buses to move as quickly and effectively as subway trains. Simultaneously, they ensured fairness by keeping fares affordable and making the system accessible to low-income residents. This balance between functionality and fairness resulted in an efficient, equitable, and sustainable public transport model that has been replicated worldwide.

On a personal level, imagine managing a group project. Balancing workload distribution (fairness) with meeting tight deadlines (efficiency) ensures that no team member feels overburdened while the group still delivers high-quality results on time.

Exercises

1. **Analyze a Trade-Off You've Made:** Reflect on a recent decision where you prioritized functionality or fairness. What was the outcome, and how could you have improved the balance between the two?

2. **Develop a Balanced Plan:** Choose a problem in your life or work (e.g. resource allocation or team management). Design a solution that maximizes both efficiency and equity.

3. **Study a Case of Utility Balancing:** Research a large-scale decision (e.g. a government program or corporate initiative). How did decision-makers balance functionality and fairness, and what lessons can you learn?

Key Takeaway

Maximizing utility means striking a balance between functionality and fairness to achieve efficient and equitable outcomes. By assessing needs, evaluating trade-offs, and crafting balanced solutions, you create sustainable progress that satisfies both practical and moral considerations.

Chapter 80: The Principle of Least Regret – Playing It Safe When Needed

Why This Matters

In life and decision-making, uncertainty is inevitable. The principle of least regret helps navigate uncertain scenarios by prioritizing choices that minimize potential negative consequences. It's a safeguard against excessive risks while still allowing for thoughtful, forward momentum. When faced with difficult decisions, this principle ensures you act rationally without being paralyzed by fear of failure.

This concept matters because regret can cloud future decision-making and harm morale. By focusing on actions that reduce regret, you gain clarity and confidence in high-stakes or uncertain environments. This principle aligns with behavioral economics concepts, such as those discussed in *Thinking, Fast and Slow* (Kahneman, 2011), which highlights how people often overestimate the pain of potential losses compared to the satisfaction of gains.

How It Works

Applying the principle of least regret involves three steps:

1. **Identify Potential Outcomes:** Map out possible consequences of each decision, including worst-case and best-case scenarios.

2. **Assess Regret Potential:** Consider which outcomes would leave you feeling the least regret if things don't go as planned.

3. **Make the Least Risky but Reasonable Choice:** Select the option that balances caution with progress, ensuring you don't overplay or underplay your hand.

This principle is particularly useful in irreversible decisions or high-stakes scenarios where outcomes can have lasting effects. In *Predictably Irrational* (Ariely, 2008), the author discusses how people often avoid risk altogether to sidestep regret but notes that calculated risk-taking with safeguards often leads to better results.

Real-Life Example

NASA's approach to the Mars Rover missions demonstrates the principle of least regret. When designing the Curiosity Rover, engineers faced the challenge of ensuring the rover could land safely on Mars, a high-risk operation with no margin for error. To minimize regret, NASA opted for a sky crane landing system that provided additional stability, even though it required more resources and innovation than simpler methods. This cautious but ambitious approach paid off, ensuring a safe landing and a successful mission.

In everyday contexts, consider an investor choosing between two opportunities: a high-risk stock and a reliable mutual fund. If the investor is more concerned about losing money than missing out on potential gains, they might opt for the mutual fund, minimizing potential regret while still making a productive choice.

Exercises

1. **Map Your Regrets:** Reflect on a recent decision that didn't go as planned. What alternative choice might have reduced your regret, and what did you learn from the experience?

2. **Simulate a Risky Decision:** Choose a hypothetical high-stakes decision. Map out the potential outcomes and apply the principle of least regret to determine the most reasonable choice.

3. **Plan for the Future:** Identify a significant decision you'll face soon. List possible options, their potential outcomes, and the choice that minimizes regret while still achieving meaningful progress.

Key Takeaway

The principle of least regret ensures you make thoughtful decisions in uncertain situations by minimizing potential negative consequences. By mapping outcomes, assessing regret potential, and choosing cautiously, you can navigate risks without sacrificing progress.

Part 9: Cultural and Ethical Dimensions of Strategy

In the realm of strategy, decisions don't exist in a vacuum—they are influenced by cultural contexts, ethical considerations, and collective values. This part explores the intersection of strategy with morality and culture, offering insights into maintaining integrity while achieving goals. From understanding unspoken norms to leveraging the wisdom of crowds, these chapters highlight the nuances of navigating global environments, balancing fairness with expediency, and making ethically sound decisions. Whether you're managing alliances, adapting to diverse cultural settings, or striving for ethical breakthroughs, this section equips you to act strategically without compromising trust or values.

Chapter 81: The Ethics of Bluffing – Getting Ahead Without Breaking Trust

Why This Matters

Bluffing is often misunderstood as deception, but when done ethically, it's a legitimate and valuable tool in strategic decision-making. The ethics of bluffing revolves around using calculated misdirection to gain leverage while respecting boundaries of trust and fairness. Ethical bluffing can help you influence outcomes, build confidence, and maintain long-term relationships.

This concept is critical because careless or dishonest bluffing can undermine credibility and harm reputations. Ethical bluffing ensures that you remain competitive without sacrificing integrity, allowing you to build trust even in high-stakes scenarios. As highlighted in *Negotiation Genius* (Malhotra & Bazerman, 2007), strategic communication and selective disclosure are central to successful and ethical bluffing.

How It Works

Ethical bluffing relies on three key principles:

1. **Understand the Context:** Bluffing is ethical when all parties understand it as part of the strategic process (e.g. negotiations or sales).

2. **Avoid Misrepresentation:** Never bluff about something that could cause harm or compromise trust if revealed.

3. **Strengthen Trust:** Use bluffing to achieve short-term leverage without damaging long-term credibility or relationships.

By following these principles, you can maintain the balance between competitive advantage and ethical responsibility.

Real-Life Example

Richard Branson's approach to launching Virgin Atlantic in the airline industry demonstrates ethical bluffing in business. When Branson announced Virgin Atlantic's launch, he strategically exaggerated the scale of the company's plans and readiness to compete with established giants like British Airways. This created buzz and positioned Virgin as a serious contender, drawing public and media attention. However, Branson avoided crossing ethical lines by ensuring that Virgin delivered a high-quality experience once the airline officially launched. The bluff succeeded in drawing interest without compromising long-term trust in the Virgin brand.

On a personal level, ethical bluffing could involve a job applicant indicating they are in talks with multiple employers. While creating urgency for a hiring decision, the bluff is ethical as long as the applicant genuinely values the opportunity being discussed.

Exercises

1. **Evaluate a Strategic Bluff:** Reflect on a time when bluffing was used in a decision-making or negotiation process. Was it ethical? What impact did it have on trust and results?

2. **Practice Ethical Bluffing:** Imagine a scenario where you need to influence someone's decision without revealing everything. Design a strategy that uses ambiguity ethically.

3. **Analyze a Corporate Strategy:** Research a company (e.g., Virgin Atlantic or another innovative player) that used bluffing or signaling. What made their strategy effective and ethical?

Key Takeaway

Bluffing can be a powerful tool when used ethically. By respecting boundaries of trust, avoiding misrepresentation, and aligning with strategic goals, you can influence outcomes while maintaining integrity and long-term credibility.

Chapter 82: Cultural Sensitivity – Adapting Processes for Global Success

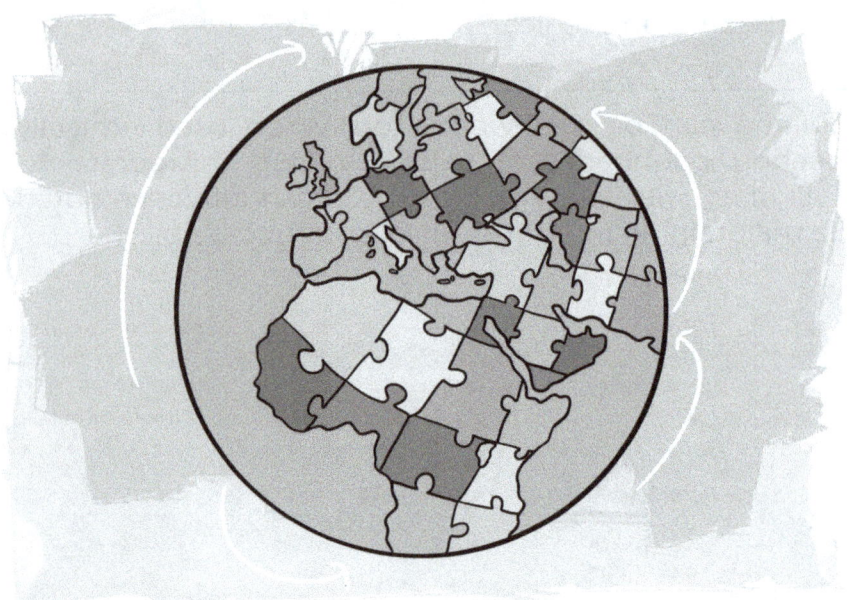

Why This Matters

In today's interconnected world, success often depends on the ability to navigate diverse cultural landscapes. Cultural sensitivity is about understanding and respecting differences in values, norms, and communication styles across cultures. Adapting processes to align with these differences enhances trust, fosters collaboration, and ensures that strategies are effective in global contexts.

This concept matters because failing to consider cultural nuances can lead to misunderstandings, conflict, and missed opportunities. As Erin Meyer explains in *The Culture Map* (2014), understanding how different cultures approach communication, decision-making, and leadership is essential for building strong international partnerships.

How It Works

Cultural sensitivity involves three key actions:

1. **Learn the Landscape:** Research the cultural norms and expectations of the people or organizations you're engaging with. This includes understanding communication styles, leadership preferences, and decision-making processes.

2. **Adapt Your Approach:** Tailor your strategies and processes to align with the cultural values of your audience. For example, some cultures prioritize consensus, while others value individual initiative.

3. **Foster Mutual Respect:** Show genuine interest in and respect for cultural differences, which builds trust and strengthens relationships.

In *When Cultures Collide* (Lewis, 2005), the author highlights how successful global leaders actively adjust their behavior to fit the cultural context, ensuring their strategies resonate across borders.

Real-Life Example

McDonald's international expansion strategy exemplifies cultural sensitivity in action. When entering markets like India, McDonald's adapted its menu to suit local tastes, introducing vegetarian options and avoiding beef-based products to respect religious and cultural norms. Similarly, in Japan, McDonald's adjusted its advertising campaigns to align with the country's emphasis on subtlety and group harmony. This ability to tailor offerings and messaging to diverse cultural contexts has been a key factor in McDonald's global success.

On a personal level, cultural sensitivity can be seen in team collaboration. For instance, a leader managing a global team might adjust their communication style to include high-context cultures (e.g. Japan) by emphasizing indirect cues while maintaining clarity for low-context cultures (e.g. Germany) through direct communication.

Exercises

1. **Cultural Research:** Choose a country or culture you're unfamiliar with. Research their business practices, communication styles, and values. Reflect on how you might adapt your approach when interacting with people from that culture.

2. **Analyze a Global Brand:** Study a company like McDonald's or Coca-Cola. How have they adapted their strategies to succeed in different cultural contexts?

3. **Practice Adapting:** Think about a recent interaction with someone from a different cultural background. What adjustments could you make to improve understanding and connection?

Key Takeaway

Cultural sensitivity is essential for global success. By learning cultural norms, adapting strategies, and fostering mutual respect, you can build strong relationships and achieve lasting impact across diverse contexts.

Chapter 83: Moral Outlining – Making a Breakthrough While Staying Ethical

Why This Matters

Pushing boundaries and achieving breakthroughs often requires challenging norms, but without ethical grounding, such progress risks harming people, reputations, or the greater good. Moral outlining is the practice of mapping out your strategic decisions within ethical boundaries. It ensures that innovation, ambition, and success remain aligned with your values and society's expectations.

This matters because short-term success achieved through unethical means often results in long-term consequences, including damaged relationships and trust. As explored in *Ethics for the Real World* (Howard & Korver, 2008), having a clear moral framework strengthens decision-making and protects against actions that might undermine integrity.

How It Works

Moral outlining involves three steps:

1. **Define Your Ethical Principles:** Establish your non-negotiables — values or actions you refuse to compromise, regardless of the situation.

2. **Assess the Impact:** Evaluate how your decisions affect stakeholders, ensuring they align with your principles and create positive outcomes.

3. **Create an Ethical Action Plan:** Build a step-by-step strategy for achieving your goals while staying within the boundaries of your moral framework.

In *The Responsible Entrepreneur* (Sharma, 2014), the author emphasizes the importance of embedding ethics into every stage of innovation, ensuring that progress serves both individual and collective goals.

Real-Life Example

Patagonia's approach to business sustainability exemplifies moral outlining. The company has consistently prioritized environmental and social responsibility over maximizing profits. For example, its "Don't Buy This Jacket" campaign encouraged customers to think twice before making unnecessary purchases, highlighting the environmental cost of consumerism. While unconventional, this strategy aligned with Patagonia's core values, strengthened customer loyalty, and reinforced its reputation as an ethical leader in the outdoor apparel industry.

On a personal level, moral outlining can be seen in decisions like turning down a lucrative but ethically questionable job offer or choosing to report unethical behavior within an organization, even when it's inconvenient or risky.

Exercises

1. **Define Your Moral Framework:** Write down your core ethical principles. How do they influence your decisions, and what actions are non-negotiable for you?

2. **Analyze an Ethical Decision:** Reflect on a time when you faced a choice between success and staying true to your values. Did you make the right decision? What did you learn from the experience?

3. **Study an Ethical Brand:** Research a company like Patagonia. How does its commitment to ethics shape its decisions and reputation?

Key Takeaway

Moral outlining ensures that breakthroughs are achieved ethically. By defining principles, assessing impacts, and creating actionable plans, you can align innovation and success with your values, building trust and lasting impact.

Chapter 84: The Invisible Rules – Understanding Unspoken Norms

Why This Matters

Success in any strategy requires not only understanding the formal rules but also recognizing the invisible, unspoken norms that govern behavior in different contexts. These "rules" may include social expectations, cultural nuances, or organizational dynamics. By understanding these subtleties, you can avoid missteps, gain influence, and strengthen relationships.

This concept is critical because ignoring unspoken norms can lead to unintended consequences, from social faux pas to broken trust. In *The Culture Map* (Meyer, 2014), the author highlights how understanding invisible rules — such as indirect communication in some cultures or hierarchical dynamics in others — is vital for building effective collaborations.

How It Works

Mastering invisible rules requires three steps:

1. **Observe Before Acting:** Take time to understand the social dynamics, cultural values, or organizational expectations in a given environment.

2. **Ask Questions Carefully:** When in doubt, seek clarification from trusted sources or colleagues to ensure you don't inadvertently break unspoken rules.

3. **Adapt and Align:** Tailor your behavior and strategies to fit the context, ensuring you operate effectively within both visible and invisible boundaries.

This approach fosters smoother interactions and avoids conflicts caused by misunderstanding or overlooking norms.

Real-Life Example

Toyota's approach to global expansion demonstrates the importance of respecting invisible rules. When Toyota entered the U.S. market, it didn't just bring its cars — it studied American consumer preferences and workplace norms. This included adapting its production methods to incorporate both Japanese efficiency principles and U.S. workers' expectations for autonomy and feedback. By respecting unspoken norms, Toyota successfully bridged cultural gaps and became one of the leading car manufacturers in the U.S.

On a personal level, understanding invisible rules might mean recognizing the unspoken dynamics in a workplace. For example, in some companies, meetings may operate informally, with decisions made in casual conversations rather than formal presentations. Recognizing and adapting to these nuances ensures smoother collaboration.

Exercises

1. **Observe a New Environment:** In a new social or professional setting, spend time observing behaviors and interactions. What unspoken norms can you identify, and how might they influence your approach?

2. **Adapt to Cultural Differences:** Research a culture you're unfamiliar with. Identify at least two unspoken norms and consider how you might adjust your behavior to align with them.

3. **Analyze a Success Story:** Study a company like Toyota or another global organization. How did they navigate unspoken norms to achieve success in new markets?

Key Takeaway

Understanding invisible rules helps you navigate unspoken norms and expectations, enabling smoother interactions and stronger relationships. By observing, asking questions, and adapting, you can build trust and operate effectively in any context.

Chapter 85: Equity vs. Expediency – Balancing Fairness in Frameworks

Why This Matters

In many strategic decisions, there's a tension between doing what's fair and doing what's fast or efficient. Equity vs. expediency highlights the challenge of balancing fairness with the need for timely and effective solutions. While fairness fosters trust and cooperation, expediency drives results. Learning to strike this balance ensures sustainable success in both leadership and collaboration.

This balance matters because leaning too far toward expediency can erode trust, while overemphasizing equity can slow progress. As highlighted in *Justice: What's the Right Thing to Do?* (Sandel, 2009), fairness and efficiency don't have to be mutually exclusive — they can coexist in a well-thought-out framework.

How It Works

Balancing equity and expediency requires three steps:

1. **Clarify Priorities:** Determine the short- and long-term goals of the situation. Is fairness critical for building trust, or does the situation demand rapid action?

2. **Evaluate Stakeholder Needs:** Identify who will be affected and how. Prioritize equity where trust and relationships are at stake, and expediency when urgency takes precedence.

3. **Find a Middle Ground:** Seek solutions that address the most pressing needs without compromising fairness entirely. Hybrid approaches often yield the best outcomes.

In *The Fifth Discipline* (Senge, 1990), systems thinking emphasizes how organizations can design frameworks that balance competing priorities, ensuring that fairness and expediency work in harmony rather than opposition.

Real-Life Example

The European Union's response to Brexit negotiations offers a compelling example of balancing equity and expediency. While the EU sought to expedite the process to minimize uncertainty, it also prioritized fairness to member states by ensuring that no single country would benefit disproportionately from the outcome. By maintaining transparency and adhering to its core principles, the EU navigated the negotiations with a balance of fairness and pragmatism.

On a smaller scale, imagine a project manager distributing tasks among team members. If one person is significantly overloaded, equity might dictate redistributing responsibilities fairly, even if it delays the project slightly. Balancing these priorities ensures both the team's morale and the project's success.

Exercises

1. **Evaluate a Past Decision:** Reflect on a time when you had to choose between equity and expediency. What was your choice, and how did it impact the outcome? How might you approach it differently?

2. **Test a Hybrid Approach:** Think of a current challenge where equity and expediency are in conflict. Develop a solution that incorporates elements of both.

3. **Analyze a Global Strategy:** Research a negotiation or initiative (e.g., Brexit or a corporate merger). How did decision-makers balance fairness with efficiency, and what were the results?

Key Takeaway

Balancing equity and expediency is key to sustainable success. By clarifying priorities, evaluating stakeholder needs, and finding middle-ground solutions, you can build trust and achieve timely results.

Chapter 86: Altruistic Choices – Sacrificing to Gain in the Long Term

TIME
ENERGY
SUPPORT

LONG-TERM GROWTH.

Why This Matters

In a competitive world, the idea of sacrificing for others may seem counterintuitive, but altruistic choices often generate trust, loyalty, and opportunities that outweigh short-term losses. By giving time, resources, or effort without expecting immediate returns, you build relationships and foster an environment of collaboration that pays dividends in the future.

This approach matters because short-sighted strategies focused solely on self-interest can damage relationships and reduce goodwill. Altruistic actions, when aligned with long-term goals, create a ripple effect of mutual benefit, as highlighted in *Give and Take* (Grant, 2014), which explores how givers often achieve greater long-term success than takers.

How It Works

Altruistic choices can lead to long-term advantages when implemented thoughtfully:

1. **Identify Meaningful Opportunities:** Focus on actions that align with your values and have the potential to create lasting positive impact.

2. **Act Without Expectation:** Approach altruism as a genuine contribution, not a transactional gesture.

3. **Build Long-Term Relationships:** Use your actions to foster trust and goodwill, ensuring that your sacrifices contribute to sustainable success.

In *The Evolution of Cooperation* (Axelrod, 1984), the concept of reciprocal altruism demonstrates how helping others can encourage mutual benefit over time, particularly in repeated interactions.

New Real-Life Example

Costco's decision to pay employees higher wages than industry standards is a powerful example of altruistic choices in business. By prioritizing employee well-being over short-term profit margins, Costco built a culture of loyalty and trust. This led to lower turnover rates, improved customer service, and a more productive workforce, which ultimately resulted in long-term financial success. Costco's actions showed that sacrificing immediate gains for the benefit of others can create sustained advantages for all parties involved.

On a personal level, altruistic choices might include volunteering time to mentor someone in your field. While it may not bring immediate rewards, the connections and goodwill generated can lead to unexpected opportunities down the road.

Exercises

1. **Reflect on a Personal Sacrifice:** Think of a time you sacrificed your own interests to help someone else. What impact did it have on them, and how did it shape your relationship or perspective?

2. **Plan a Meaningful Action:** Identify a way you can support someone in your personal or professional life. Focus on an action that aligns with your values and creates positive impact.

3. **Research an Example:** Study a company or leader that made an altruistic decision, such as Costco. How did their actions benefit others, and what long-term success did they achieve?

Key Takeaway

Altruistic choices can create significant long-term gains by fostering trust, loyalty, and collaboration. By sacrificing strategically and focusing on meaningful actions, you build relationships and opportunities that lead to sustainable success.

Chapter 87: Historical Lessons – Learning from Great Minds

Why This Matters

The challenges of today often mirror those of the past. Learning from great minds in history provides invaluable insights into strategy, resilience, and decision-making. Whether navigating political turmoil, advancing innovation, or solving complex social problems, historical figures often faced similar dilemmas, offering lessons that remain relevant today.

This approach matters because ignoring history risks repeating mistakes. By studying how great leaders overcame challenges, you can extract practical strategies and apply them in modern contexts, as highlighted in *Leadership in War* (Roberts, 2019), which explores the decision-making processes of historical leaders during crises.

How It Works

Drawing lessons from history involves three steps:

1. **Identify Parallels:** Look for historical events or figures that faced challenges similar to yours. Focus on their strategies and thought processes.

2. **Analyze Their Choices:** Examine what worked, what didn't, and why. Understand how their context influenced their decisions.

3. **Apply the Principles:** Adapt the lessons to fit your unique circumstances, ensuring they align with modern challenges and opportunities.

In *The Lessons of History* (Durant & Durant, 1968), the authors emphasize the recurring nature of human behavior and decisions, making history a valuable guide for solving contemporary problems.

Real-Life Example

Abraham Lincoln's leadership during the U.S. Civil War exemplifies the value of historical lessons. Faced with a deeply divided nation, Lincoln prioritized clear communication, moral clarity, and long-term vision to preserve the Union. His decision to issue the Emancipation Proclamation — while controversial — was both a moral and strategic act that strengthened the North's position while undermining the Confederacy. Today, leaders can draw from Lincoln's example to navigate complex negotiations, manage crises, and inspire others through purpose-driven leadership.

On a smaller scale, studying a figure like Marie Curie — who persevered despite significant societal barriers to make ground-breaking scientific discoveries — can inspire resilience and determination in personal and professional pursuits.

Exercises

1. **Research a Historical Leader:** Choose a historical figure whose challenges resonate with your own. Study their strategies and reflect on how their lessons can apply to your situation.

2. **Analyze a Historical Event:** Identify a major event (e.g., the Civil War or the Industrial Revolution). What strategies were employed, and how can they inform modern decisions?

3. **Create a Personal Connection:** Write down a challenge you're currently facing. Identify a historical parallel and outline three lessons you can apply.

Key Takeaway

History offers a treasure trove of strategic insights. By studying the decisions of great minds, you can adapt their lessons to modern challenges, ensuring informed, effective, and purpose-driven action.

Chapter 88: Managing Alliances – Balancing Loyalty and Pragmatism

Why This Matters

Strategic alliances amplify resources, expertise, and opportunities, but they require careful management to balance loyalty and pragmatism. Managing alliances is about nurturing trust and cooperation while ensuring that the partnership remains aligned with your evolving objectives. Strong alliances can propel success, while poorly managed ones can become liabilities.

This concept matters because alliances often face challenges like shifting priorities or unequal contributions. Balancing loyalty to the partnership with a practical approach ensures that collaborations remain mutually beneficial. As explored in *Collaborating with the Enemy* (Kahane, 2017), successful partnerships thrive on clear communication, adaptability, and a shared vision.

How It Works

Managing alliances effectively involves three key principles:

1. **Define Shared Goals:** Clearly establish the partnership's objectives, ensuring they align with the interests of all parties.

2. **Communicate Transparently:** Regular communication fosters trust, helps address conflicts early, and keeps the alliance adaptable to change.

3. **Know When to Pivot:** Balance loyalty to the alliance with the need to adjust or exit when the partnership no longer serves its purpose.

These steps create a foundation for strong alliances that are both resilient and flexible, ensuring long-term success.

Real-Life Example

The strategic partnership between Spotify and Waze highlights the balance of loyalty and pragmatism in alliances. In 2017, the companies joined forces to integrate music streaming with navigation, providing users with seamless control of Spotify playlists within the Waze app. This collaboration benefited both platforms — Spotify gained exposure to Waze users, while Waze enhanced its user experience with music functionality. Despite the partnership, both companies retained their independence and pursued their broader business goals, demonstrating how alliances can thrive through alignment and mutual benefit without overdependence.

On a personal level, managing alliances might look like collaborating with a colleague on a shared project while maintaining the flexibility to pursue individual career goals. Clear communication and mutual respect ensure that both parties benefit from the partnership.

Exercises

1. **Evaluate an Alliance:** Reflect on a partnership you've been involved in. What aspects of the alliance worked well, and where could there have been better alignment or communication?

2. **Build an Alliance Strategy:** Identify a potential partner in your personal or professional life. Outline shared goals, define communication methods, and establish how you'll balance loyalty with pragmatism.

3. **Analyze a Partnership:** Study the Spotify-Waze partnership or another alliance. What strategies did they use to align their goals and maintain balance, and what can you learn from their approach?

Key Takeaway

Managing alliances requires balancing loyalty with pragmatism. By fostering trust, maintaining transparency, and knowing when to pivot, you can create partnerships that drive shared success and adaptability.

Chapter 89: Ethical Negotiation – Advancing Without Exploiting

Why This Matters

Negotiation often involves conflicting interests, but the true art lies in advancing your goals without exploiting others. Ethical negotiation focuses on achieving outcomes that benefit all parties while maintaining trust, fairness, and long-term relationships. It ensures that success is built on collaboration, not coercion, and protects your reputation in future dealings.

This matters because exploitative tactics may yield short-term wins but often result in damaged relationships, loss of trust, and reputational harm. As discussed in *Getting to Yes* (Fisher & Ury, 1981), principled negotiation fosters creative, win-win solutions that align with ethical standards and mutual interests.

How It Works

Ethical negotiation involves three critical practices:

1. **Focus on Interests, Not Positions:** Identify the underlying needs and priorities of all parties rather than rigid demands. This opens pathways for creative solutions.

2. **Be Transparent and Honest:** Share relevant information openly while respecting confidentiality, ensuring fairness without compromising your position.

3. **Seek Win-Win Outcomes:** Strive for agreements that leave all parties satisfied, fostering goodwill and long-term collaboration.

This approach ensures that negotiation is a constructive process that strengthens relationships rather than undermining them.

Real-Life Example

The 1993 Oslo Accords between Israel and the Palestine Liberation Organization (PLO) exemplify ethical negotiation in a high-stakes context. Facilitated by Norway, the negotiations focused on mutual recognition and peaceful coexistence. Although not without flaws, the accords were built on principles of fairness and shared interests, such as land rights and self-governance. The process emphasized transparency, mutual respect, and a focus on common goals, demonstrating that even deeply divided parties can find common ground through ethical negotiation.

On a smaller scale, consider a salary negotiation. An ethical approach involves being honest about your expectations, understanding the employer's constraints, and finding a solution—like additional benefits or growth opportunities—that meets both parties' needs.

Exercises

1. **Reflect on a Negotiation:** Think about a past negotiation you participated in. Was it conducted ethically? What could have been done differently to improve the process and outcome?

2. **Practice Interests-Based Negotiation:** Role-play a negotiation scenario with a partner. Focus on identifying each other's interests and developing a solution that satisfies both parties.

3. **Analyze a Historic Agreement:** Research the Oslo Accords or another major negotiation. What strategies were employed to achieve fairness, and what lessons can you apply?

Key Takeaway

Ethical negotiation is about advancing goals without exploitation. By focusing on interests, fostering transparency, and seeking win-win outcomes, you can achieve success while building trust and long-term relationships.

Chapter 90: The Wisdom of Crowds – Leveraging Collective Intelligence

Why This Matters

Harnessing the power of collective intelligence can transform decision-making and innovation. The wisdom of crowds leverages the combined knowledge, perspectives, and creativity of a group to solve complex problems, predict outcomes, and generate groundbreaking ideas. Properly structured, this approach outperforms even the most talented individuals by pooling insights and reducing biases.

This matters because relying on a single viewpoint, no matter how informed, limits possibilities. As James Surowiecki explores in *The Wisdom of Crowds* (2004), when groups are diverse, independent, and aggregated effectively, they consistently produce superior outcomes in fields ranging from business to science.

How It Works

For the wisdom of crowds to work effectively, three principles must be followed:

1. **Encourage Diversity:** Include participants with varied expertise, experiences, and perspectives to broaden the knowledge base.

2. **Promote Independent Thinking:** Allow each contributor to express their insights freely, without being swayed by others.

3. **Aggregate Input Effectively:** Use systems or tools to compile, analyze, and synthesize the group's contributions into actionable solutions.

This approach fosters creativity and robust decision-making while mitigating individual biases.

Real-Life Example

NASA's "Mars Exploration Rover" public contest demonstrates the power of collective intelligence. Before sending the Spirit and Opportunity rovers to Mars in 2003, NASA invited students across the United States to participate in a naming contest. Thousands of submissions poured in, reflecting the creativity and thoughtfulness of young minds. The winning names — Spirit and Opportunity — not only resonated with NASA's mission but also generated public engagement and enthusiasm for the Mars program. This example illustrates how collective contributions, even from unexpected sources, can lead to meaningful outcomes.

On a smaller scale, businesses can use employee suggestion programs to solve internal challenges. For instance, Toyota's "Kaizen" philosophy encourages workers at all levels to contribute ideas for process improvements, leading to innovation and operational efficiency.

Exercises

1. **Host a Problem-Solving Session:** Gather a diverse group to brainstorm solutions to a challenge you're facing. Use structured methods, like the Delphi technique, to aggregate and refine their input.

2. **Analyze a Collective Achievement:** Research a successful use of collective intelligence (e.g. NASA's naming contest or Toyota's Kaizen system). What principles were applied, and what can you learn from them?

3. **Crowdsource Feedback:** Use a survey or online poll to collect ideas or opinions from a larger group. Reflect on how these aggregated insights could inform your decisions.

Key Takeaway

The wisdom of crowds harnesses collective intelligence to solve problems, innovate, and make better decisions. By fostering diversity, independence, and effective aggregation, you can unlock the full potential of group contributions.

Part 10: Mastering the Game of Life

In life, the stakes are high, the players are diverse, and the rules are ever-changing. Mastering the game of life requires more than talent or luck—it demands strategy, resilience, and an unwavering commitment to growth. This final section explores how game theory principles can be applied to personal and professional development, empowering you to thrive amidst uncertainty, build lasting connections, and leave a meaningful legacy. Whether you're navigating setbacks, influencing others, or playing for the long term, these chapters will provide the tools to strategize for success and fulfillment in every dimension of your life.

Chapter 91: Personal Plans – Applying Game Theory to Your Life

Why This Matters

Life is filled with decisions that shape your path, from career moves to relationships and personal growth. Applying game theory to your personal plans helps you make smarter, more intentional choices by analyzing potential outcomes, considering others' actions, and optimizing strategies for success.

This matters because hasty or unexamined decisions can lead to regret or missed opportunities. Using game theory principles enables you to think several steps ahead, anticipate obstacles, and align your actions with your long-term goals.

How It Works

Applying game theory to your life involves three steps:

1. **Identify Your Goals:** Define what success looks like for you in different areas of life (e.g. financial stability, strong relationships, personal fulfillment).

2. **Map Possible Outcomes:** Consider the choices available to you and predict how others' actions might influence your path. Use tools like decision trees to visualize scenarios.

3. **Strategize for Optimal Results:** Choose the path that maximizes your gains while minimizing risks, ensuring alignment with your values and long-term vision.

In *Thinking in Bets* (Duke, 2018), the author emphasizes how strategic thinking improves decision-making by incorporating probabilities and potential outcomes, even when uncertainty is present.

Real-Life Example

Oprah Winfrey's career decisions illustrate personal planning rooted in strategic thinking. When transitioning from her talk show to building a media empire, Oprah weighed her options carefully, considering the risks and rewards of launching the Oprah Winfrey Network (OWN). By aligning her actions with her vision of empowering others and diversifying her brand, she maximized her long-term success while navigating complex decisions.

Exercises

1. **Define Your Life Game Plan:** Choose a major decision you're facing. Use game theory principles to map out potential scenarios and identify the optimal choice.

2. **Study a Strategic Career Move:** Research a leader like Oprah Winfrey or another public figure. How did their decisions align with game theory principles, and what can you learn from their approach?

3. **Create a Decision Tree:** Visualize a personal choice by outlining possible actions, their outcomes, and the factors influencing each option. Reflect on which path aligns best with your goals.

Key Takeaway

Applying game theory to your personal plans enables you to make intentional, strategic decisions. By analyzing outcomes, anticipating others' actions, and aligning choices with your goals, you can chart a course for success and fulfillment.

Chapter 92: Handling Uncertainty – Thriving in the Unknown

Why This Matters

Uncertainty is a constant in life, whether in careers, relationships, or personal goals. Handling uncertainty means embracing the unknown and making decisions confidently despite incomplete information. Learning to thrive in unpredictable situations builds resilience, creativity, and adaptability, allowing you to seize opportunities and navigate challenges with clarity.

This matters because fear of uncertainty often leads to indecision or overly cautious choices. As Nassim Nicholas Taleb discusses in *Antifragile* (2012), uncertainty can be a source of growth and innovation if approached with the right mindset and strategy.

How It Works

Thriving in uncertainty involves three key strategies:

1. **Focus on Controllable Actions:** Identify what you can influence and take deliberate steps to move forward, even when the outcome isn't guaranteed.

2. **Build Flexibility:** Stay open to adjusting your plans as new information emerges, ensuring you can pivot when necessary.

3. **Adopt a Growth Mindset:** View uncertainty as an opportunity to learn and grow rather than a source of fear.

By focusing on these strategies, you can reduce the anxiety of the unknown and harness its potential for personal and professional growth.

Real-Life Example

The rapid response of Zoom during the COVID-19 pandemic showcases thriving in uncertainty. As demand for remote communication tools surged unexpectedly, Zoom quickly adapted by scaling its infrastructure, prioritizing security updates, and launching user-friendly features. Despite the unpredictable circumstances, the company's agility allowed it to meet the needs of millions of users worldwide, solidifying its position as a market leader.

On a personal level, thriving in uncertainty might look like pursuing a new career path despite lacking all the details upfront. By taking small, intentional steps—such as networking or gaining relevant skills—you can move forward while remaining adaptable.

Exercises

1. **Identify Controllables:** Think about an uncertain situation you're facing. Write down the aspects you can influence and create a plan to address them.

2. **Practice Flexibility:** Reflect on a time when a plan didn't go as expected. How did you adapt, and what could you do differently next time to handle uncertainty more effectively?

3. **Analyze an Agile Organization:** Study a company like Zoom or another leader that thrived during a period of uncertainty. What strategies did they use, and how can you apply similar principles in your life?

Key Takeaway

Uncertainty is inevitable, but it doesn't have to be paralyzing. By focusing on controllable actions, building flexibility, and embracing a growth mindset, you can turn unpredictability into a source of strength and opportunity.

Chapter 93: Targeted Storytelling – Persuasion Through a Specific Script

Why This Matters

Storytelling isn't just an art — it's a strategy. Targeted storytelling uses specific, purpose-driven narratives to persuade and inspire others. A well-told story connects emotionally, simplifies complex ideas, and motivates action, making it an essential tool for communication and influence.

This matters because data alone rarely drives decisions; it's the emotional connection that compels people to act. As explored in *Made to Stick* (Heath & Heath, 2007), stories that are clear, specific, and relatable are far more persuasive than facts presented in isolation.

How It Works

Effective targeted storytelling involves three steps:

1. **Understand Your Audience:** Tailor your narrative to the needs, values, and emotions of the people you're addressing.

2. **Focus on Specifics:** Use concrete details and examples to make your story relatable and memorable.

3. **End with a Call to Action:** Ensure your story inspires the audience to think, feel, or act in alignment with your goals.

By mastering these steps, you can craft compelling stories that resonate and drive meaningful outcomes.

Real-Life Example

Nike's "Just Do It" campaign demonstrates the power of targeted storytelling. Rather than simply promoting athletic products, Nike tells stories of perseverance and triumph, featuring athletes of all levels overcoming challenges. These narratives inspire customers by connecting deeply with their aspirations and emotions, turning Nike into a brand synonymous with determination and success.

On a personal level, targeted storytelling might involve sharing a specific example of how a past project succeeded to persuade a team to adopt your approach for a new initiative. The right story can clarify your vision and rally others behind it.

Exercises

1. **Craft a Personal Story:** Think of a challenge you've overcome. Write a short narrative with specific details and a clear message to share with someone who might benefit from your experience.

2. **Analyze an Effective Campaign:** Study a storytelling-based marketing campaign, such as Nike's. What made it effective, and how can you apply similar techniques in your communication?

3. **Tailor a Story to Your Audience:** Choose a professional or personal goal you're working toward. Develop a story that aligns with your audience's values and inspires them to support your vision.

Key Takeaway

Targeted storytelling is a powerful way to influence and inspire. By tailoring your narratives, focusing on specifics, and driving action, you can connect with others on a deeper level and achieve your goals.

Chapter 94: Building Resilience – Recovering from Setbacks

Why This Matters

Setbacks are inevitable, but resilience — the ability to recover and grow stronger in the face of adversity — is what separates temporary failure from long-term success. Building resilience equips you with the mental and emotional tools to adapt, persevere, and thrive when things go wrong.

This matters because life's challenges often test your resolve, and how you respond determines your trajectory. In *Grit* (Duckworth, 2016), Angela Duckworth emphasizes that persistence, combined with adaptability, is a critical factor in achieving success over time.

How It Works

Building resilience involves three core practices:

1. **Reframe Setbacks as Opportunities:** View failures not as permanent losses but as valuable learning experiences that can guide your future actions.

2. **Develop Coping Mechanisms:** Cultivate habits like mindfulness, journaling, or physical activity to process stress and maintain focus.

3. **Foster a Support Network:** Surround yourself with people who encourage, challenge, and inspire you, providing a safety net when setbacks occur.

By practicing these steps, you can transform difficulties into stepping stones for growth and progress.

Real-Life Example

Howard Schultz's journey with Starbucks demonstrates the power of resilience. When Schultz joined Starbucks in the 1980s, the company faced financial struggles, and his vision of turning it into a global coffee empire was met with doubt. Despite numerous rejections and challenges, Schultz persevered, refining his strategy and securing funding. Today, Starbucks is one of the most recognizable brands worldwide, largely due to Schultz's ability to recover and learn from setbacks.

On a personal level, resilience might mean bouncing back from a failed job interview or business pitch by seeking feedback, refining your approach, and trying again with renewed determination.

Exercises

1. **Reframe a Recent Setback:** Think about a challenge you've faced recently. What lessons can you take from the experience, and how can you apply them moving forward?

2. **Strengthen Your Coping Mechanisms:** Identify one habit—like mindfulness or journaling—you can develop to process stress and improve focus. Practice it for a week and reflect on the impact.

3. **Analyze a Resilient Leader:** Study someone like Howard Schultz or another public figure known for resilience. What strategies did they use to recover from setbacks, and how can you incorporate them into your own life?

Key Takeaway

Resilience is about transforming setbacks into opportunities for growth. By reframing challenges, developing coping mechanisms, and fostering a strong support network, you can recover stronger and achieve lasting success.

Chapter 95: Continuous Improvement – Learning from Every Situation

KEEP REFINING

Why This Matters

Life is a constant journey of growth, but improvement doesn't happen automatically — it requires deliberate effort. Continuous improvement means reflecting on each experience, identifying lessons, and applying those insights to evolve over time. This practice helps you adapt, innovate, and achieve lasting success.

This matters because success is often built on incremental progress rather than grand leaps. As outlined in *Atomic Habits* (Clear, 2018), small, consistent changes compound over time to produce transformational results.

How It Works

To integrate continuous improvement into your life, follow these three steps:

1. **Reflect on Outcomes:** After any experience, evaluate what went well and what could have been done differently.

2. **Embrace Feedback:** Actively seek constructive input from others to gain new perspectives and identify blind spots.

3. **Take Action and Adjust:** Implement changes based on your reflections and feedback, continuously refining your approach.

By committing to these steps, you create a cycle of growth that strengthens your skills, knowledge, and resilience.

Real-Life Example

Pixar Animation Studios exemplifies continuous improvement through its commitment to refining the creative process. After completing each film, Pixar holds a "post-mortem" session where the team dissects what worked and what didn't, from storytelling to technical execution. These lessons inform their next project, allowing Pixar to consistently deliver innovative and emotionally resonant films. This iterative process has been key to their success, producing hits like *Toy Story* and *Inside Out*.

On a personal level, continuous improvement might involve analyzing how you prepared for a big presentation. By reflecting on what aspects resonated with your audience and what could be enhanced, you can refine your approach for even greater impact in the future.

Exercises

1. **Reflect on a Recent Event:** Choose a recent experience or project you worked on. Identify two things you did well and one thing you could improve. Write down how you'll address this in the future.

2. **Ask for Constructive Feedback:** Reach out to someone you trust and ask for their input on a skill or project you're working on. Use their suggestions to create a specific action plan for improvement.

3. **Track Small Changes Over Time:** Choose one habit or behavior to improve (e.g., time management or communication). Track your progress over the next month, making small adjustments each week. Reflect on how these changes add up.

Key Takeaway

Continuous improvement transforms experiences into opportunities for growth. By reflecting, seeking feedback, and taking deliberate action, you can refine your approach and achieve lasting progress in all areas of your life.

Chapter 96: The Mastery of Perspective – Seeing the Big Picture

Why This Matters

In life, it's easy to get lost in the details and lose sight of the larger vision. Mastering perspective means learning to zoom out and see the overarching patterns, connections, and long-term implications of decisions. It's about aligning day-to-day actions with a broader strategy, ensuring clarity and focus in your pursuits.

This concept matters because short-term thinking often leads to missed opportunities or mistakes that could have been avoided with a bigger-picture view. In *The Art of Thinking Clearly* (Dobelll, 2013), the author emphasizes the importance of avoiding cognitive biases that limit perspective and focusing on long-term goals instead.

How It Works

Mastering perspective involves three essential practices:

1. **Zoom Out:** Regularly step back to evaluate how your current actions align with your broader goals.

2. **Seek Diverse Insights:** Incorporate viewpoints from others to gain a more comprehensive understanding of the situation.

3. **Balance Macro and Micro Views:** Alternate between the big picture and key details to ensure your strategy is cohesive and actionable.

By cultivating this skill, you can make decisions that are not only effective in the moment but also contribute to long-term success.

Real-Life Example

Satya Nadella's leadership at Microsoft illustrates the mastery of perspective. When Nadella became CEO in 2014, he shifted Microsoft's focus from short-term profits to long-term growth by prioritizing cloud computing, artificial intelligence, and cross-platform collaboration. This required a big-picture view of the industry's future and the willingness to make strategic changes. His vision transformed Microsoft into one of the world's most valuable companies while fostering innovation and adaptability.

On a personal level, mastering perspective might involve balancing career goals with personal well-being. For instance, someone overly focused on work might zoom out to recognize the importance of health and relationships, adjusting their priorities accordingly.

Exercises

1. **Zoom Out on a Current Goal:** Choose a goal or project you're working on. Reflect on how it fits into your broader vision for your life or career. What adjustments could you make to better align with your long-term objectives?

2. **Gather Diverse Perspectives:** Discuss a major decision with trusted friends, colleagues, or mentors. Compare their views with your own and consider how their insights might shape your understanding.

3. **Balance Micro and Macro Views:** Practice alternating between the big picture and specific details of a current challenge. How do these perspectives complement each other, and how can they inform your strategy?

Key Takeaway

Mastering perspective allows you to align daily actions with long-term goals. By zooming out, seeking diverse insights, and balancing macro and micro views, you can make informed decisions that lead to sustainable success.

Chapter 97: Focused Networking – Expanding Your Sphere of Influence

Why This Matters

In a world driven by collaboration, relationships are one of the most valuable assets. Focused networking emphasizes building meaningful, strategic connections rather than chasing quantity. By aligning your relationships with your goals and values, you create a support system that fosters personal and professional growth.

This matters because a scattershot approach to networking often results in shallow, unproductive relationships. As Porter Gale explains in *Your Network Is Your Net Worth* (2013), meaningful connections lead to greater opportunities and deeper collaboration than superficial interactions.

How It Works

Building a focused network requires three steps:

1. **Identify Key Connections:** Determine the individuals or groups whose values and goals align with yours, and prioritize building relationships with them.

2. **Foster Genuine Relationships:** Approach networking with authenticity, focusing on mutual benefit rather than self-interest.

3. **Maintain Your Network:** Regularly engage with your connections through meaningful interactions to keep relationships strong and mutually beneficial.

This approach ensures that your network is both supportive and effective in helping you achieve your goals.

Real-Life Example

Reid Hoffman, co-founder of LinkedIn, exemplifies focused networking. Hoffman's success stems from his ability to cultivate meaningful relationships with other tech leaders, investors, and innovators. By aligning his connections with his vision of fostering professional collaboration, Hoffman built not only a robust network but also a platform that revolutionized how people connect professionally.

On a personal level, focused networking might mean identifying mentors who can guide your career or colleagues who share your vision for a project. Building these relationships authentically ensures long-term support and collaboration.

Exercises

1. **Map Your Network:** Create a list of your current connections. Identify which relationships align most closely with your goals and focus on nurturing those connections.

2. **Reach Out Strategically:** Identify one person in your desired field or industry you'd like to connect with. Reach out with a thoughtful message explaining why you value their work and how you can mutually benefit.

3. **Strengthen Existing Relationships:** Choose three people in your network to reconnect with. Schedule a coffee chat or send a personalized message to catch up and offer support.

Key Takeaway

Focused networking builds meaningful connections that align with your goals and values. By prioritizing key relationships, fostering authenticity, and maintaining engagement, you can expand your sphere of influence and open doors to new opportunities.

Chapter 98: Balancing Solutions and Tactics – Knowing When to Zoom In

Why This Matters

In problem-solving, knowing when to focus on detailed tactics versus overarching solutions is critical. Balancing solutions and tactics means understanding when to prioritize high-level strategy and when to zero in on the specific actions needed to execute that strategy. This balance ensures that your efforts are both effective and aligned with your long-term goals.

This matters because too much focus on tactics can lead to micromanagement, while an exclusive focus on solutions can result in inaction or poorly executed plans. As highlighted in *The McKinsey Way* (Rasiel, 1999), the best problem-solvers move fluidly between strategic thinking and actionable steps.

How It Works

Balancing solutions and tactics involves three essential steps:

1. **Define the Problem Clearly:** Start by identifying whether the challenge requires a high-level solution, a tactical approach, or both.

2. **Move Between Levels as Needed:** Regularly assess whether you need to zoom out for perspective or zoom in to address specific challenges.

3. **Ensure Alignment:** Confirm that your tactics serve the larger solution, creating coherence between your immediate actions and long-term goals.

This dynamic approach ensures that no detail is overlooked while maintaining focus on the bigger picture.

Real-Life Example

SpaceX's Mars mission planning demonstrates the balance between solutions and tactics. The overarching solution is to establish a sustainable human presence on Mars, a goal requiring visionary strategy. At the same time, SpaceX tackles tactical challenges like improving rocket reusability and refining spacecraft design to bring this vision closer to reality. By aligning these detailed actions with their big-picture goal, SpaceX progresses steadily toward its ambitious mission.

On a personal level, this balance could involve developing a five-year career plan (solution) while taking specific steps like upskilling or networking (tactics) to ensure progress toward your broader vision.

Exercises

1. **Analyze a Current Goal:** Identify a goal you're working toward. Map out the high-level solution and the detailed tactics required to achieve it. How well are these two levels aligned?

2. **Switch Perspectives:** Choose a current challenge and practice alternating between focusing on the broader solution and the specific tactics. Reflect on how shifting perspectives helps refine your approach.

3. **Study a Balanced Strategy:** Research a company like SpaceX or another organization known for strategic innovation. How do they balance long-term solutions with short-term tactics?

Key Takeaway

Balancing solutions and tactics ensures effective problem-solving. By defining the problem, moving between levels as needed, and aligning tactics with overarching goals, you can achieve sustainable success.

Chapter 99: Legacy Planning – Going Beyond the Current Status Quo

Why This Matters

Legacy isn't just about what you leave behind—it's about the values, achievements, and influence you create that endure beyond your time. Legacy planning involves thinking long-term, ensuring that your efforts contribute to a lasting impact that benefits others and aligns with your purpose.

This matters because focusing solely on immediate success can limit your potential for making a meaningful, enduring contribution. As Stephen R. Covey explains in *The 7 Habits of Highly Effective People* (1989), beginning with the end in mind ensures that your actions today align with the legacy you want to leave tomorrow.

How It Works

Effective legacy planning involves three key principles:

1. **Define Your Values and Purpose:** Clarify what matters most to you and how you want to be remembered.

2. **Align Actions with Long-Term Impact:** Ensure that your decisions and efforts contribute to a greater goal beyond immediate outcomes.

3. **Empower Others:** Build systems or relationships that allow your influence to grow and continue after you're gone.

This approach helps you create a legacy that reflects your values and drives positive change.

Real-Life Example

Bill and Melinda Gates' philanthropic efforts through the Gates Foundation exemplify legacy planning. By dedicating their resources to global health, education, and poverty reduction, they've created a foundation that will continue to make an impact for generations. Their focus on sustainability and long-term goals ensures that their work extends beyond their lifetimes.

On a personal level, legacy planning could involve mentoring someone who can carry forward your values and vision or contributing to a cause that aligns with your purpose.

Exercises

1. **Define Your Legacy:** Reflect on how you want to be remembered. Write down your core values and how they align with the impact you want to create.

2. **Plan for Long-Term Impact:** Identify one action you can take today that will contribute to a lasting legacy. This could be creating a mentorship program, starting a community initiative, or writing a book to share your knowledge.

3. **Study an Inspiring Legacy:** Research a figure like Bill Gates or another individual known for their enduring contributions. What steps did they take to ensure their work would outlast them, and what lessons can you apply?

Key Takeaway

Legacy planning is about creating an enduring impact that reflects your values and purpose. By defining what matters, aligning your actions, and empowering others, you can build a legacy that inspires and influences beyond your lifetime.

Chapter 100: Infinite Games – Thriving in a World Without End

THE GAME NEVER ENDS

Why This Matters

Many of life's challenges and pursuits aren't finite—they don't have a clear endpoint or a fixed set of rules. Infinite games, as described by Simon Sinek in *The Infinite Game* (2019), require a mindset of adaptability, resilience, and continuous evolution. Thriving in such a world means focusing on growth, relationships, and purpose rather than "winning."

This matters because playing with a finite mindset in an infinite game often leads to burnout, short-term thinking, and unsustainable results. Adopting an infinite mindset ensures that you stay relevant, impactful, and fulfilled over the long haul, no matter how the rules or circumstances change.

How It Works

Thriving in infinite games involves three key shifts in mindset:

1. **Focus on Vision, Not Victory:** Embrace a purpose that guides your actions over the long term, rather than short-term achievements.

2. **Prioritize Relationships:** Build connections that endure and evolve, creating a strong support network for sustained success.

3. **Adapt to Change:** Treat challenges as opportunities to grow and redefine your approach, staying flexible in the face of uncertainty.

These principles allow you to navigate the complexities of life's infinite games while remaining grounded in your values and vision.

Real-Life Example

The evolution of Patagonia under Yvon Chouinard's leadership exemplifies the infinite game mindset. Rather than focusing solely on profit, Patagonia prioritizes environmental sustainability and social responsibility. This long-term vision has allowed the company to thrive and remain relevant for decades, building loyal customer relationships and inspiring other businesses to adopt similar practices. By committing to a purpose beyond short-term wins, Patagonia demonstrates how infinite thinking creates lasting impact.

On a personal level, embracing infinite games could mean pursuing lifelong learning or focusing on relationships that grow and evolve over time, rather than viewing success as a single destination.

Exercises

1. **Identify Your Infinite Game:** Reflect on an area of your life — such as career, relationships, or personal growth — where success doesn't have a fixed endpoint. What purpose or vision can guide your long-term actions?

2. **Strengthen Long-Term Relationships:** Choose one relationship you value deeply. Plan a meaningful way to nurture and grow that connection, prioritizing its longevity over immediate outcomes.

3. **Adapt to a Challenge:** Think of a recent obstacle you've faced. How can you approach it with a mindset of growth and flexibility, seeing it as part of an ongoing journey rather than a finite win or loss?

Key Takeaway

In a world of infinite games, success isn't about winning — it's about staying adaptable, purpose-driven, and committed to growth. By focusing on vision, relationships, and flexibility, you can thrive in a world without end.

Conclusion

Strategy is more than a tool — it is a lens through which the complexities of life become navigable. Every decision, whether large or small, fits into an interconnected game with players, rules, and outcomes. This book has revealed how the principles of game theory illuminate pathways for navigating challenges, optimizing decisions, and achieving meaningful goals.

Through foundational ideas such as the **Prisoner's Dilemma** and **Tit-for-Tat**, collaboration emerged as a dominant force, often more powerful than competition. Concepts like **Pareto Efficiency** and the **Nash Equilibrium** demonstrated the balance between individual and collective benefit, offering insights into building stable, mutually advantageous outcomes. These tools are not confined to theory but serve as practical frameworks for daily decisions.

Navigating Complexity with Advanced Tools

Moving from foundational concepts to advanced strategies, the book emphasized tools for thriving in an uncertain and dynamic world. Techniques like **Bayesian Touchpoints** and **Scenario Analysis** equipped decision-makers to operate effectively despite incomplete information, while ideas like **Entry Deterrence** and **Competitive Positioning** provided the means to stay ahead in competitive environments.

Strategies such as **Backward Induction** and **Resource Management** also highlighted the importance of balancing big-picture vision with precise, tactical action. The interplay of these perspectives ensures that each decision is not only effective in isolation but aligned with long-term goals.

Ethics, Culture, and Long-Term Thinking

In a world that increasingly values trust and inclusion, game theory demonstrated its relevance in navigating human dynamics. The chapters on **Ethical Negotiation**, **Cultural Sensitivity**, and **Moral Outlining** showed how strategic thinking can harmonize with integrity. Far from being rigid, these strategies adapt to the nuances of cultural differences and ethical dilemmas, ensuring sustainable and respectful success.

Beyond external achievements, the book shifted focus inward, guiding readers toward personal mastery. Strategies like the **Win-Win Mindset**, **Infinite Games**, and **Legacy Planning** reinforced the importance of long-term thinking. These tools emphasized that life is not a series of isolated victories but an ongoing pursuit of growth, resilience, and impact.

The Ripple Effect of Decisions

Game theory teaches that every decision creates ripples. These ripples influence systems, relationships, and future opportunities. Understanding the rules of the game, anticipating others' moves, and aligning choices with overarching goals allows for intentional actions that shape meaningful outcomes.

Through the mastery of tactics such as **Bluffing and Signaling**, **Managing Alliances**, and **Building Resilience**, this book empowered decision-makers to navigate complexity with clarity. Tools like **Continuous Improvement** and **Scenario Analysis** underscored the importance of adapting and learning from each challenge, turning setbacks into opportunities for growth.

Embracing the Infinite Game

The ultimate lesson of game theory is that life is not a finite game with clear winners and losers. Instead, it is an infinite game, where the goal is to thrive, adapt, and create lasting value. This requires vision, patience, and a willingness to evolve. Success is not measured by short-term gains but by the ability to sustain purpose and impact over time.

The game of life is dynamic, complex, and filled with possibilities. The strategies outlined in this book offer a toolkit for mastering its challenges. The next move is yours to make. Play it wisely.

Appendix A: Quick Reference Guide

This appendix serves as a streamlined guide to the 100 chapters of *Game Theory: An AI's Guide to 100 Strategies for Mastering Decisions, Negotiations, and Human Dynamics*. Designed for ease of navigation, each chapter title is accompanied by a concise one-liner summarizing its essence. Use this section to revisit specific strategies, refresh your understanding, or quickly locate tools relevant to your needs.

Part 1: Foundations of Strategic Thinking

1. **The Prisoner's Dilemma**: Explore the tension between cooperation and defection in competitive scenarios.
2. **Tit-for-Tat**: Learn the power of reciprocity to foster long-term collaboration.
3. **Dominant Strategies**: Identify the best decision regardless of others' actions.
4. **Pareto Efficiency**: Discover how to maximize mutual gains in decision-making.
5. **Nash Equilibrium**: Achieve stability where no player benefits from unilateral changes.
6. **Zero-Sum Games**: Succeed in situations where one's gain is another's loss.
7. **Non-Zero-Sum Games**: Create shared wins through collaborative problem-solving.

8. **Backward Induction**: Master planning by thinking ahead and acting backward.
9. **The Stag Hunt**: Balance risk and reward in collaborative efforts.
10. **The Ultimatum Scenario**: Weigh fairness and self-interest in negotiations.

Part 2: Advanced Tactics for Decision-Making

11. **Mixed Tactics**: Use calculated randomness to outwit predictable opponents.
12. **Minimax Programs**: Guard against the worst-case scenario in any strategy.
13. **Commitment Devices**: Solidify your resolve through strategic pre-commitments.
14. **Schelling Points**: Coordinate actions with unspoken agreements.
15. **Shapley Value**: Divide resources fairly in complex situations.
16. **Bluffing and Signaling**: Deploy deception effectively while maintaining credibility.
17. **Opportunity Cost**: Recognize the trade-offs in every decision.
18. **First-Mover Advantage**: Gain the upper hand by leading strategically.
19. **Stackelberg Leadership**: Dominate by taking calculated leadership positions.
20. **Sequential Interplays**: Leverage the long game in decision-making chains.

Part 3: Winning in Negotiations

21. **BATNA**: Develop a strong exit plan to negotiate with confidence.
22. **Anchoring Effect**: Set the tone early by framing initial offers strategically.
23. **Logrolling**: Exchange concessions for maximum mutual benefit.

24. **ZOPA**: Identify the zone of possible agreement to close deals.
25. **Splitting the Difference**: Master the art of compromise to move forward.
26. **Hardball Tactics**: Stand firm under pressure without losing leverage.
27. **Framing Effects**: Shape narratives to influence outcomes.
28. **The Decoy Effect**: Guide choices by introducing strategic alternatives.
29. **Supremacy Dynamics**: Exploit strengths and minimize weaknesses effectively.
30. **Deadline Master Plan**: Use timing as a negotiation weapon.

Part 4: Navigating Human Dynamics

31. **Social Proof**: Lead by leveraging group consensus.
32. **Contextualizing**: Redefine the rules to gain strategic advantages.
33. **Moral Hazards**: Avoid creating incentives for harmful behavior.
34. **The Tragedy of the Commons**: Protect shared resources through smart governance.
35. **The Sunk Cost Fallacy**: Let go of losses and focus on future value.
36. **Information Asymmetry**: Manage gaps in knowledge to your benefit.
37. **Herd Behavior**: Anticipate and influence group dynamics.
38. **Reputation Capital**: Build and use trust wisely in strategic moves.
39. **Shadow of the Future**: Make decisions with long-term consequences in mind.
40. **Overconfidence Bias**: Avoid the pitfalls of hubris in planning.

Part 5: Resilient and Creative Strategies

41. **Redundancy**: Prepare for failure by building buffers.

42. **Flexible Approaches**: Adapt to real-time changes for sustained success.

43. **Scenario Analysis**: Plan for multiple potential outcomes.

44. **Win-Win Mindset**: Expand opportunities to benefit everyone involved.

45. **Emotional Regulation**: Maintain composure under fire.

46. **Empathy Mapping**: Understand others' motivations to strategize effectively.

47. **Asymmetric Warfare**: Win with fewer resources through unconventional strategies.

48. **Coalition Building**: Strengthen your position by building alliances.

49. **Resource Management**: Prioritize and optimize for efficiency.

50. **Leverage Longevity**: Achieve greater returns through patience.

Part 6: Strategies for Handling Complexity

51. **Multi-Party Negotiations**: Manage competing interests in group dynamics.

52. **Design Approach**: Set the stage for strategic success.

53. **Bayesian Touchpoints**: Make informed decisions with incomplete information.

54. **The Value of Patience**: Delay immediate action for larger rewards.

55. **Escalation Control**: Prevent destructive spirals in conflicts.

56. **Evolutionary Methods**: Adapt strategies as rules change.

57. **Hybrid Blueprints**: Blend synergy and competition for strategic gains.

58. **Liability Diversification**: Spread risks to achieve stability.

59. **The Cost of Complexity**: Simplify systems to remain competitive.

60. **Behavioral Insights**: Use psychology to gain an edge.

Part 7: Game Theory in Everyday Life

61. **Negotiating with Irrational Players**: Stay calm when facing unpredictable behavior.
62. **Frictionless Output**: Eliminate barriers to streamline teamwork.
63. **Timing the Market**: Master the art of acting at the right moment.
64. **Repetition and Reputation**: Achieve long-term success through consistent actions.
65. **Incentive Alignment**: Motivate others by aligning goals and rewards.
66. **Loss Aversion**: Turn fear of loss into strategic opportunity.
67. **Prospect Theory**: Reframe challenges to improve decision-making.
68. **The Role of Luck**: Acknowledge and manage uncontrollable factors.
69. **Trust Building**: Create lasting alliances by fostering credibility.
70. **The Domino Effect**: Anticipate and influence chain reactions in decision-making.

Part 8: Advanced Game Theory Applications

71. **The Superior Mindset**: Think like a master player for strategic advantage.
72. **The Role of Information**: Control the flow of knowledge to shape outcomes.
73. **Credible Threats**: Leverage authority without direct action.
74. **Counterfactual Reasoning**: Prepare for "what if" scenarios and future moves.
75. **Signaling Power**: Communicate strength through strategic messaging.
76. **Competitive Positioning**: Stand out in a crowded market with unique value.

77. **Entry Deterrence**: Protect your territory by discouraging rivals.

78. **Managing Missteps**: Turn failures into learning opportunities.

79. **Maximizing Utility**: Balance fairness and functionality in decision-making.

80. **The Principle of Least Regret**: Minimize risks when outcomes are uncertain.

Part 9: Cultural and Ethical Dimensions of Strategy

81. **The Ethics of Bluffing**: Advance strategically while maintaining trust.

82. **Cultural Sensitivity**: Adapt strategies for global success.

83. **Moral Outlining**: Break through challenges without compromising ethics.

84. **The Invisible Rules**: Navigate unspoken norms and hidden structures.

85. **Equity vs. Expediency**: Balance fairness with efficiency in complex systems.

86. **Altruistic Choices**: Make sacrifices for long-term gains.

87. **Historical Lessons**: Apply insights from great thinkers to modern strategy.

88. **Managing Alliances**: Weigh loyalty and pragmatism in partnerships.

89. **Ethical Negotiation**: Progress without exploiting others.

90. **The Wisdom of Crowds**: Harness collective intelligence for innovation.

Part 10: Mastering the Game of Life

91. **Personal Plans**: Use game theory to optimize daily decisions.

92. **Handling Uncertainty**: Thrive amidst unpredictable circumstances.

93. **Targeted Storytelling**: Persuade effectively with a clear and specific narrative.

94. **Building Resilience**: Recover and grow stronger after setbacks.

95. **Continuous Improvement**: Learn and refine from every experience.

96. **The Mastery of Perspective**: Balance the immediate and the big picture.

97. **Focused Networking**: Build influence through meaningful connections.

98. **Balancing Solutions and Tactics**: Know when to zoom in or out for clarity.

99. **Legacy Planning**: Shape a future that extends beyond current achievements.

100. **Infinite Games**: Adopt a mindset of thriving in a limitless journey.

Appendix B: Chapter Overview by Section

This appendix provides a streamlined breakdown of the book's structure, listing all sections and their respective chapters in an easy-to-navigate format. Use this guide as a quick reference to locate specific topics or revisit key strategies covered in the book.

Part 1: Foundations of Strategic Thinking

- The Prisoner's Dilemma: Cooperation vs. Defection
- Tit-for-Tat: The Power of Reciprocity
- Dominant Strategies: Choosing the Best Option
- Pareto Efficiency: Maximizing Mutual Gains
- Nash Equilibrium: Finding Stability in Structures
- Zero-Sum Games: Succeeding at Someone Else's Expense
- Non-Zero-Sum Games: Shared Triumphs through Working Together
- Backward Induction: Thinking Ahead, Acting Backward
- The Stag Hunt: Risk and Reward in Collaboration
- The Ultimatum Scenario: Balancing Fairness and Self-Interest

Part 2: Advanced Tactics for Decision-Making

- Mixed Tactics: Embracing Calculated Randomness
- Minimax Programs: Guarding Against the Worst-Case
- Commitment Devices: Strengthening Your Resolve
- Schelling Points: Unspoken Agreements in Coordination
- Shapley Value: Fair Divisions in Complex Situations
- Bluffing and Signaling: The Art of Deception
- Opportunity Cost: Recognizing What You Sacrifice
- First-Mover Advantage: Leading for Personal Gain
- Stackelberg Leadership: Dominating by Taking the Lead
- Sequential Interplays: Playing the Long Game

Part 3: Winning in Negotiations

- BATNA: Always Have an Exit Plan
- Anchoring Effect: Setting the Tone Early
- Logrolling: Trading Concessions for Maximum Gains
- ZOPA: Identifying the Zone of Possible Agreement
- Splitting the Difference: Mastering Compromise
- Hardball Tactics: Standing Firm Against Pressure
- Framing Effects: Shaping the Narrative to Win
- The Decoy Effect: Steering Choices Subtly
- Supremacy Dynamics: Using Strong Points and Weakness
- Deadline Master Plan: Using Time as Leverage

Part 4: Navigating Human Dynamics

- Social Proof: Leading with Consensus
- Contextualizing: Define the Rules to Trump the System
- Moral Hazards: Avoid Incentivizing Bad Behavior
- The Tragedy of the Commons: Protecting Shared Resources
- The Sunk Cost Fallacy: Knowing When to Let Go

Part 7: Game Theory in Everyday Life

- Negotiating with Irrational Players: Keeping Calm Under Chaos
- Frictionless Output: Reducing Barriers to Teamwork
- Timing the Market: Knowing When to Act
- Repetition and Reputation: Reaching Your Goals Through Consistency
- Incentive Alignment: Motivating Others Effectively
- Loss Aversion: Turning Fear into Opportunity
- Prospect Theory: Seeing Challenges the Right Way
- The Role of Luck: Managing the Uncontrollable
- Trust Building: Creating Long-Term Alliances
- The Domino Effect: Anticipating Chain Reactions

Part 8: Advanced Game Theory Applications

- The Superior Mindset: Act Like a Master Player
- The Role of Information: Controlling the Flow for Victory
- Credible Threats: Using Authority Without Acting
- Counterfactual Reasoning: What If and What Next?
- Signaling Power: Sending the Right Messages
- Competitive Positioning: Standing Out in Crowded Markets
- Entry Deterrence: Keeping Rivals Out of Your Territory
- Managing Missteps: Learning from Failures
- Maximizing Utility: Balancing Functionality and Fairness
- The Principle of Least Regret: Playing It Safe When Needed

Part 9: Cultural and Ethical Dimensions of Strategy

- The Ethics of Bluffing: Getting Ahead Without Breaking Trust
- Cultural Sensitivity: Adapting Processes for Global Success

Appendix C: Practice Scenarios

This appendix presents real-world scenarios where the strategies discussed in this book can be applied to solve challenges effectively. Each scenario highlights a specific problem and explains how certain game theory strategies can help address the issue. By working through these scenarios, readers can strengthen their ability to apply theoretical concepts to practical situations.

Scenario 1: Launching a New Product in a Crowded Market

Problem: A small start-up is preparing to launch a new product in an industry dominated by well-established players. The team is worried about how to differentiate their offering and gain consumer attention without substantial marketing resources.

Applicable Strategies:

- **Competitive Positioning (Chapter 76):** To stand out, the start-up must identify its unique value proposition—what makes its product different from and better than competitors'.

- **Entry Deterrence (Chapter 77):** By positioning aggressively, such as offering unique features or competitive pricing, the start-up can deter competitors from attempting to replicate or outshine its product.

- **Signaling Power (Chapter 75):** The start-up can use bold but credible claims, such as emphasizing limited availability or highlighting innovation, to create intrigue and attract early adopters.

Scenario 2: Negotiating a High-Stakes Partnership

Problem: Two companies with complementary strengths are negotiating a strategic partnership. However, conflicting priorities—one side wants immediate profits, while the other is focused on long-term value—are creating friction.

Applicable Strategies:

- **BATNA (Chapter 21):** Each company should develop strong alternatives to strengthen their negotiation position. Knowing they have other options can provide leverage.

- **ZOPA (Chapter 24):** Both parties must identify the Zone of Possible Agreement by understanding the overlap between their minimum acceptable outcomes.

- **Splitting the Difference (Chapter 25):** As a last resort, a fair compromise can help bridge the gap, ensuring both parties see value in moving forward.

Scenario 3: Handling an Unpredictable Competitor

Problem: A competitor in your industry has been making erratic moves, such as price cuts and surprise product launches, creating uncertainty and disruption for your company's strategy.

Applicable Strategies:

- **Mixed Tactics (Chapter 11):** Introducing calculated randomness into your actions can make your strategy less predictable and harder for competitors to counter.

- **Negotiating with Irrational Players (Chapter 61):** Rather than reacting impulsively, stay calm and focus on actions that align with your long-term goals, regardless of the competitor's behavior.

- **Framing Effects (Chapter 27):** Shape the narrative of the situation in your favor, emphasizing your strengths and stability to reassure customers and partners.

Scenario 4: Resolving a Workplace Conflict

Problem: Two employees have conflicting approaches to solving a critical project problem. The disagreement is escalating, delaying progress and lowering morale.

Applicable Strategies:

- **Emotional Regulation (Chapter 45):** As a leader, staying calm and managing your emotions will allow you to mediate effectively without escalating the conflict further.

- **Empathy Mapping (Chapter 46):** Understanding each employee's motivations and concerns can help identify common ground and guide the team toward a collaborative solution.

- **Social Proof (Chapter 31):** Highlighting examples of successful teamwork from the past can remind the team of the benefits of collaboration and inspire a cooperative mindset.

Scenario 5: Balancing Short-Term and Long-Term Goals

Problem: A CEO must decide whether to pursue a quick financial gain that would temporarily boost quarterly earnings or focus on a long-term investment that would take years to pay off but could secure the company's future.

Applicable Strategies:

- **Shadow of the Future (Chapter 39):** Long-term planning must take precedence, as decisions made today will influence the company's reputation and sustainability tomorrow.

- **The Value of Patience (Chapter 54):** Delaying immediate rewards in favor of larger returns later demonstrates strategic foresight and builds resilience.

- **Infinite Games (Chapter 100):** The goal is not to win short-term battles but to remain a significant player in the industry for years to come.

Scenario 6: Expanding into a Global Market

Problem: A company entering a foreign market struggles to navigate cultural differences and adapt its operations to local norms.

Applicable Strategies:

- **Cultural Sensitivity (Chapter 82):** Understanding and respecting cultural nuances ensures smoother communication and operations.

- **Contextualizing (Chapter 32):** Redefine internal processes to align with the rules and expectations of the new market.

- **Information Asymmetry (Chapter 36):** Bridge knowledge gaps by gathering detailed local insights to make informed decisions.

Scenario 7: Negotiating a Tight Deadline

Problem: Your team is negotiating with a supplier who is delaying key materials needed for a time-sensitive product launch. Without the materials, the launch could fail.

Applicable Strategies:

- **Deadline Master Plan (Chapter 30):** Use the impending deadline as leverage to push the supplier to prioritize your order. Highlight the consequences of delays to emphasize urgency.

- **Hardball Tactics (Chapter 26):** Apply firm but fair pressure to ensure the supplier understands the seriousness of the situation while protecting the long-term relationship.

- **Credible Threats (Chapter 73):** If necessary, signal that alternative suppliers are available and ready to step in, providing the leverage to secure action.

Scenario 8: Encouraging Team Innovation

Problem: A team's creative output has plateaued, and they are struggling to generate new ideas or solve ongoing challenges effectively.

Applicable Strategies:

- **Flexible Approaches (Chapter 42):** Encourage an iterative process where team members can experiment with unconventional methods without fear of failure.
- **Scenario Analysis (Chapter 43):** Introduce structured brainstorming by analyzing multiple "what-if" scenarios to stimulate creative thinking.
- **Building Resilience (Chapter 94):** Foster a culture where setbacks during innovation are treated as learning opportunities, building the team's confidence to explore bolder ideas.

Scenario 9: Preventing Resource Overload

Problem: A manager notices the team's workload is increasing beyond their capacity, leading to inefficiencies and burnout.

Applicable Strategies:

- **Resource Management (Chapter 49):** Assess and prioritize tasks to focus on what delivers the highest value while eliminating or delegating non-essential work.
- **Redundancy (Chapter 41):** Build buffers into the team's processes by assigning backup resources to critical tasks.
- **The Cost of Complexity (Chapter 59):** Simplify workflows and remove unnecessary layers of complexity to improve productivity and reduce stress.

Scenario 10: Addressing Public Backlash Over a Controversy

Problem: A brand has made a decision that triggered negative public reactions. Rebuilding trust with its audience is critical to preserving its market position.

Applicable Strategies:

- **Reputation Capital (Chapter 38):** Leverage existing goodwill and transparency to communicate your response effectively. Highlight prior commitments to social responsibility or customer care.

- **Ethical Negotiation (Chapter 89):** Engage with stakeholders, including critics, to address concerns openly and find solutions that restore credibility.
- **The Wisdom of Crowds (Chapter 90):** Use public feedback to demonstrate active listening and ensure future decisions are better aligned with expectations.

Scenario 11: Creating a Long-Term Alliance

Problem: Two organizations want to collaborate on a multi-year initiative, but differing priorities and distrust complicate discussions.

Applicable Strategies:

- **Managing Alliances (Chapter 88):** Develop a clear agreement that balances loyalty with flexibility to adapt over time.
- **Trust Building (Chapter 69):** Foster credibility through consistent communication, transparency, and delivering small, mutual wins early in the collaboration.
- **Multi-Party Negotiations (Chapter 51):** Use structured dialogue to ensure both parties' needs are met while navigating conflicts.

Scenario 12: Anticipating Consumer Behavior Trends

Problem: A company wants to predict consumer preferences to stay ahead of its competitors, but market data is inconclusive.

Applicable Strategies:

- **Herd Behavior (Chapter 37):** Observe patterns of group dynamics and consumer behavior to identify emerging trends.
- **Behavioral Insights (Chapter 60):** Apply psychological principles to analyze why consumers make certain choices.
- **Timing the Market (Chapter 63):** Use predictive models to act at the right moment when trends begin to solidify.

Scenario 13: Responding to an Aggressive Competitor

Problem: A rival company has aggressively cut prices and launched targeted marketing campaigns, threatening your market share.

Applicable Strategies:

- **Asymmetric Warfare (Chapter 47):** Focus on niche strengths or unconventional tactics to counter the competitor's actions without engaging directly.
- **Entry Deterrence (Chapter 77):** Reinforce your market position by improving customer loyalty and locking in distribution channels.
- **Bluffing and Signaling (Chapter 16):** Send signals that you are prepared to match their actions, such as through pricing or promotions, even if you don't fully commit.

Scenario 14: Simplifying a Complex System

Problem: A project involves multiple stakeholders, competing priorities, and intricate processes that slow progress and increase costs.

Applicable Strategies:

- **The Cost of Complexity (Chapter 59):** Identify and eliminate redundancies in the project's design to streamline processes.
- **Design Approach (Chapter 52):** Reorganize the project using first principles to create a foundation that promotes efficiency and clarity.
- **Pareto Efficiency (Chapter 4):** Focus on solutions that provide maximum mutual benefit with minimal compromises.

Scenario 15: Deciding When to Walk Away

Problem: You're stuck in a negotiation that is becoming increasingly unbalanced, with diminishing returns despite continued effort and resources.

Applicable Strategies:

- **BATNA (Chapter 21):** Evaluate your best alternative to the current deal, ensuring you're prepared to walk away confidently.

- **The Sunk Cost Fallacy (Chapter 35):** Avoid letting previous investments dictate your decisions. Focus on future benefits rather than past losses.

- **The Principle of Least Regret (Chapter 80):** Prioritize the option that minimizes long-term regret, even if it means stepping back now.

Appendix D: Strategic Checklist

This strategic checklist is designed as a practical tool for applying the principles and strategies covered in this book. By following these checkpoints, readers can systematically evaluate their decisions, identify opportunities, and address challenges effectively. Each checkpoint includes actionable steps to ensure no detail is overlooked. Use this guide as a foundation for strategic thinking in any situation.

1. Define Your Objective Clearly

- Identify your primary goal and desired outcome.
- Ensure the objective aligns with your long-term vision or values.
- Break the goal into smaller, actionable milestones.

2. Understand the Stakes

- Assess the risks and rewards associated with the decision.
- Identify potential consequences of success or failure.
- Prioritize based on the impact of each possible outcome.

3. Map Out the Players

- List all key stakeholders and their interests.
- Identify allies, competitors, and neutral parties.
- Analyze the motivations and goals of each player.

4. Evaluate Available Resources

- Take inventory of time, money, and personnel available.
- Identify gaps in resources and plan how to fill them.
- Optimize current assets to stretch their impact.

5. Assess Your Alternatives

- Define your BATNA (Best Alternative to a Negotiated Agreement).
- Brainstorm multiple pathways to achieve the objective.
- Rank alternatives based on feasibility and impact.

6. Anticipate Opposing Moves

- Think like your competitor or adversary — what would they do next?
- Identify potential threats or disruptions.
- Develop counterstrategies for each anticipated move.

7. Build Trust Strategically

- Establish credibility through transparency and consistency.
- Identify ways to deliver small wins to build goodwill.
- Use empathy and active listening to strengthen alliances.

8. Simplify Complexity

- Remove unnecessary steps or elements from the process.
- Focus on the 20% of actions that deliver 80% of results (Pareto principle).
- Communicate clearly and concisely to avoid misunderstandings.

9. Leverage Timing Effectively

- Identify the best time to act for maximum impact.
- Use deadlines to create urgency or gain leverage.
- Be patient when waiting for the right opportunity to emerge.

10. Stay Flexible

- Embrace an adaptive mindset to respond to unexpected changes.
- Test small changes before committing to large-scale shifts.
- Always have a contingency plan for critical actions.

11. Use Data Wisely

- Gather and analyze reliable data to inform decisions.
- Cross-check assumptions against factual evidence.
- Avoid analysis paralysis by focusing on actionable insights.

12. Frame the Narrative

- Shape how others perceive the situation to align with your goals.
- Highlight benefits and mitigate perceived risks in your messaging.
- Use storytelling to create a compelling and persuasive argument.

13. Manage Emotions

- Recognize emotional triggers in yourself and others.
- Maintain composure, even under pressure or provocation.
- Use empathy to defuse tensions and build rapport.

14. Think Long-Term

- Evaluate how today's decisions will impact future outcomes.
- Avoid short-term wins that could lead to long-term losses.
- Invest in strategies that build sustainable success.

15. Learn from Setbacks

- Conduct a post-mortem analysis after every failure or misstep.
- Identify lessons that can improve future decision-making.
- Use setbacks as stepping stones to refine your strategy.

Pro Tip: The Rule of 3

Always ask these three questions before making a critical decision:

1. What am I trying to achieve?
2. Who will be affected, and how?
3. How does this align with my long-term goals?

These three guiding questions can sharpen focus, reduce distractions, and ensure every decision contributes to lasting success.

Appendix E: Resources

1. Akerlof, George A. (1970). *The Market for Lemons: Quality Uncertainty and the Market Mechanism.* Quarterly Journal of Economics.

2. Ariely, Dan. (2008). *Predictably Irrational: The Hidden Forces That Shape Our Decisions.* Harper Perennial.

3. Arrow, Kenneth J. (1974). *The Limits of Organization.* W.W. Norton & Company.

4. Axelrod, Robert. (1984). *The Evolution of Cooperation.* Basic Books.

5. Banerjee, Abhijit V. (1992). *A Simple Model of Herd Behavior.* Quarterly Journal of Economics.

6. Bazerman, Max H., and Neale, Margaret A. (1992). *Negotiating Rationally.* The Free Press.

7. Beinhocker, Eric D. (2006). *The Origin of Wealth: Evolution, Complexity, and the Radical Remaking of Economics.* Harvard Business Review Press.

8. Benartzi, Shlomo, and Thaler, Richard H. (2004). *Save More Tomorrow: Using Behavioral Economics to Increase Employee Saving.* Journal of Political Economy.

9. Berger, Jonah. (2013). *Contagious: Why Things Catch On.* Simon & Schuster.

10. Berne, Eric. (1964). *Games People Play: The Psychology of Human Relationships.* Grove Press.

11. Bezos, Jeff. (1997). *Shareholder Letter.* Amazon.com.

12. Brandenburger, Adam, and Nalebuff, Barry. (1996). *Co-opetition: A Revolutionary Mindset That Combines Competition and Cooperation.* Currency Doubleday.

13. Brown, Brené. (2018). *Dare to Lead: Brave Work. Tough Conversations. Whole Hearts.* Random House.

14. Buffett, Warren. (2013). *The Giving Pledge.* GivingPledge.org.

15. Camerer, Colin, and Loewenstein, George. (2014). *Behavioral Economics and Public Policy.* Princeton University Press.

16. Catmull, Ed, and Wallace, Amy. (2014). *Creativity, Inc.: Overcoming the Unseen Forces That Stand in the Way of True Inspiration.* Random House.

17. Catmull, Ed. (2014). *Creativity, Inc.: Overcoming the Unseen Forces That Stand in the Way of True Inspiration.* Random House.

18. Chouinard, Yvon. (2005). *Let My People Go Surfing: The Education of a Reluctant Businessman.* Penguin Books.

19. Christensen, Clayton M. (1997). *The Innovator's Dilemma: When New Technologies Cause Great Firms to Fail.* Harvard Business School Press.

20. Cialdini, Robert B. (1984). *Influence: The Psychology of Persuasion.* Harper Business.

21. Clausewitz, Carl von. (1832). *On War.* Princeton University Press (translated editions).

22. Clear, James. (2018). *Atomic Habits: An Easy & Proven Way to Build Good Habits & Break Bad Ones.* Avery.

23. Clear, James. (2018). *Atomic Habits: An Easy & Proven Way to Build Good Habits & Break Bad Ones.* Avery.

24. Covey, Stephen M.R. (2006). *The Speed of Trust: The One Thing That Changes Everything.* Free Press.

25. Covey, Stephen R. (1989). *The 7 Habits of Highly Effective People: Powerful Lessons in Personal Change.* Free Press.

26. Dearlove, Des. (2007). *Business the Richard Branson Way: 10 Secrets of the World's Greatest Brand Builder.* Capstone Publishing.

27. Diermeier, Daniel. (2011). *Reputation Rules: Strategies for Building Your Company's Most Valuable Asset.* McGraw-Hill Education.

28. Dixit, Avinash, and Nalebuff, Barry. (1991). *Thinking Strategically: The Competitive Edge in Business, Politics, and Everyday Life.* W.W. Norton & Company.

29. Dobelli, Rolf. (2013). *The Art of Thinking Clearly.* Harper.

30. Drucker, Peter F. (1967). *The Effective Executive.* Harper & Row.

31. Duckworth, Angela. (2016). *Grit: The Power of Passion and Perseverance.* Scribner.

32. Duhigg, Charles. (2012). *The Power of Habit: Why We Do What We Do in Life and Business.* Random House.

33. Duke, Annie. (2018). *Thinking in Bets: Making Smarter Decisions When You Don't Have All the Facts.* Portfolio.

34. Durant, Will, and Ariel Durant. (1968). *The Lessons of History.* Simon & Schuster.

35. Dweck, Carol S. (2006). *Mindset: The New Psychology of Success.* Ballantine Books.

36. Dyson, James. (2000). *Against the Odds: An Autobiography.* Texere.

37. Elster, Jon. (1979). *Ulysses and the Sirens: Studies in Rationality and Irrationality.* Cambridge University Press.

38. European Union. (2020). *Brexit Negotiation Frameworks and Agreements.* Official Reports Archive.

39. Fehr, Ernst, and Schmidt, Klaus M. (1999). *A Theory of Fairness, Competition, and Cooperation.* Quarterly Journal of Economics.

40. Fisher, Roger, and Ury, William. (1981). *Getting to Yes: Negotiating Agreement Without Giving In.* Penguin Books.

41. Fisher, Roger, and Ury, William. (1981). *Getting to Yes: Negotiating Agreement Without Giving In.* Penguin Books.

42. Fudenberg, Drew, and Tirole, Jean. (1991). *Game Theory.* MIT Press.

43. Gale, Porter. (2013). *Your Network Is Your Net Worth: Unlock the Hidden Power of Connections for Wealth, Success, and Happiness.* Atria Books.

44. Gates, Bill, and Gates, Melinda. (2021). *Gates Foundation Annual Report.* Gates Foundation Archives.

45. Gawande, Atul. (2009). *The Checklist Manifesto: How to Get Things Right.* Metropolitan Books.

46. Gawer, Annabelle, and Cusumano, Michael A. (2002). *Platform Leadership: How Intel, Microsoft, and Cisco Drive Industry Innovation.* Harvard Business School Press.

47. Gibbons, Robert. (1992). *A Primer in Game Theory.* Prentice Hall.

48. Gladwell, Malcolm. (2000). *The Tipping Point: How Little Things Can Make a Big Difference.* Little, Brown and Company.

49. Godin, Seth. (2003). *Purple Cow: Transform Your Business by Being Remarkable.* Portfolio.

50. Goldstein, Noah J., Martin, Steve J., and Cialdini, Robert B. (2008). *Yes! 50 Scientifically Proven Ways to Be Persuasive.* Free Press.

51. Goleman, Daniel. (1995). *Emotional Intelligence: Why It Can Matter More Than IQ.* Bantam Books.

52. Goodwin, Doris Kearns. (2005). *Team of Rivals: The Political Genius of Abraham Lincoln.* Simon & Schuster.

53. Graham, Benjamin. (1949). *The Intelligent Investor.* Harper Business.

54. Grant, Adam. (2014). *Give and Take: Why Helping Others Drives Our Success.* Penguin Books.

55. Greenblatt, Joel. (2010). *The Little Book That Still Beats the Market.* Wiley.

56. Greene, Robert. (1998). *The 48 Laws of Power.* Penguin Books.

57. Gross, James J. (2014). *Handbook of Emotion Regulation.* The Guilford Press.

58. Güth, Werner, Schmittberger, Rolf, and Schwarze, Bernd. (1982). *An Experimental Analysis of Ultimatum Bargaining.* Journal of Economic Behavior & Organization.

59. Hardin, Garrett. (1968). *The Tragedy of the Commons.* Science.

60. Hardy, Darren. (2010). *The Compound Effect: Jumpstart Your Income, Your Life, Your Success.* Vanguard Press.

61. Harvard Business Review. (2003). *The Power of Negotiation: Mastering Negotiation Strategies.* Harvard Business School Press.

62. Heath, Chip, and Heath, Dan. (2007). *Made to Stick: Why Some Ideas Survive and Others Die.* Random House.

63. Heath, Chip, and Heath, Dan. (2007). *Made to Stick: Why Some Ideas Survive and Others Die.* Random House.

64. Hoffman, Reid. (2014). *The Start-Up of You: Adapt to the Future, Invest in Yourself, and Transform Your Career.* Currency.

65. Holling, C.S. (1973). *Resilience and Stability of Ecological Systems.* Annual Review of Ecology and Systematics.

66. Hollnagel, Erik. (2011). *Resilience Engineering in Practice: A Guidebook.* Ashgate Publishing.

67. Howard, Ronald A., and Korver, Clinton D. (2008). *Ethics for the Real World: Creating a Personal Code to Guide Decisions in Work and Life.* Harvard Business Review Press.

68. Imai, Masaaki. (1986). *Kaizen: The Key to Japan's Competitive Success.* McGraw-Hill Education.

69. Intel Corporation. (2020). *Annual Report and Market Analysis*

70. Isaacson, Walter. (2011). *Steve Jobs.* Simon & Schuster.

71. Jobs, Steve. (2005). *Stanford Commencement Address.*

72. Kahane, Adam. (2017). *Collaborating with the Enemy: How to Work with People You Don't Agree with or Like or Trust.* Berrett-Koehler Publishers.

73. Kahneman, Daniel, and Tversky, Amos. (1979). *Prospect Theory: An Analysis of Decision under Risk.* Econometrica.

74. Kahneman, Daniel, and Tversky, Amos. (1981). *The Framing of Decisions and the Psychology of Choice.* Science.

75. Kahneman, Daniel. (2011). *Thinking, Fast and Slow.* Farrar, Straus and Giroux.

76. Kelley, Tom. (2001). *The Art of Innovation: Lessons in Creativity from IDEO, America's Leading Design Firm.* Crown Business.

77. Lax, David A., and Sebenius, James K. (1986). *The Manager as Negotiator: Bargaining for Cooperation and Competitive Gain.* The Free Press.

78. Lencioni, Patrick. (2002). *The Five Dysfunctions of a Team: A Leadership Fable.* Jossey-Bass.

79. Leonard, Thomas C. (2016). *Illiberal Reformers: Race, Eugenics, and American Economics in the Progressive Era.* Princeton University Press.

80. Lewis, Michael. (2016). *The Undoing Project: A Friendship That Changed Our Minds.* W.W. Norton & Company.

81. Lewis, Richard D. (2005). *When Cultures Collide: Leading Across Cultures.* Nicholas Brealey Publishing.

82. Lewis, Richard D. (2005). *When Cultures Collide: Leading Across Cultures.* Nicholas Brealey Publishing.

83. Lieberman, Marvin B., and Montgomery, David B. (1988). *First-Mover Advantages.* Strategic Management Journal.

84. Liedtka, Jeanne, and Ogilvie, Tim. (2011). *Designing for Growth: A Design Thinking Tool Kit for Managers.* Columbia Business School Publishing.

85. Lincoln, Abraham. (1953). *The Collected Works of Abraham Lincoln.* Edited by Roy P. Basler.

86. Luce, R. Duncan, and Raiffa, Howard. (1957). *Games and Decisions: Introduction and Critical Survey.* Wiley.

87. Maeda, John. (2006). *The Laws of Simplicity: Design, Technology, Business, Life.* MIT Press.

88. Malhotra, Deepak, and Bazerman, Max H. (2008). *Negotiation Genius: How to Overcome Obstacles and Achieve Brilliant Results at the Bargaining Table and Beyond.* Bantam.

89. Malkiel, Burton G. (2003). *A Random Walk Down Wall Street: The Time-Tested Strategy for Successful Investing.* W.W. Norton & Company.

90. Mankiw, N. Gregory. (1998). *Principles of Economics.* Cengage Learning.

91. Mauboussin, Michael J. (2012). *The Success Equation: Untangling Skill and Luck in Business, Sports, and Investing.* Harvard Business Review Press.

92. Maxwell, John C. (2007). *Failing Forward: Turning Mistakes into Stepping Stones for Success.* Thomas Nelson.

93. McKeown, Greg. (2014). *Essentialism: The Disciplined Pursuit of Less.* Crown Business.

94. McKeown, Greg. (2014). *Essentialism: The Disciplined Pursuit of Less.* Crown Business.

95. McRaney, David. (2011). *You Are Not So Smart: Why You Have Too Many Friends on Facebook, Why Your Memory Is Mostly Fiction, and 46 Other Ways You're Deluding Yourself.* Gotham Books.

96. Meadows, Donella H. (2008). *Thinking in Systems: A Primer.* Chelsea Green Publishing.

97. Meyer, Erin. (2014). *The Culture Map: Breaking Through the Invisible Boundaries of Global Business.* PublicAffairs.

98. Meyer, Erin. (2014). *The Culture Map: Breaking Through the Invisible Boundaries of Global Business.* PublicAffairs.

99. Musk, Elon. (2021). *SpaceX Mission Updates.* SpaceX Official Blog.

100. Myerson, Roger B. (1991). Game Theory: Analysis of Conflict. Harvard University Press.

101. Nadella, Satya. (2017). *Hit Refresh: The Quest to Rediscover Microsoft's Soul and Imagine a Better Future for Everyone.* Harper Business.

102. NASA. (1986). *Rogers Commission Report on the Challenger Accident.*

103. NASA. (2003). *Girl with Dreams Names Mars Rovers 'Spirit' and 'Opportunity'.* NASA Archives.

104. NASA. (2012). *Mars Science Laboratory (Curiosity) Mission Overview.*

105. Nash, John F. (1950). *Equilibrium Points in n-Person Games.* Proceedings of the National Academy of Sciences.

106. National Transportation Safety Board (NTSB). (1912). *Titanic Disaster Report.*

107. Nike. (1988). *"Just Do It" Campaign Archive.* Nike Archives.

108. Ostrom, Elinor. (1990). *Governing the Commons: The Evolution of Institutions for Collective Action.* Cambridge University Press.

109. Ostrom, Elinor. (2009). *Nobel Prize Lecture: Beyond Markets and States: Polycentric Governance of Complex Economic Systems.*

110. Ostrom, Elinor. (2010). *Governing the Commons: The Evolution of Institutions for Collective Action.* Cambridge University Press.

111. Pareto, Vilfredo. (1906). *Manual of Political Economy.* Macmillan Publishing.

112. Patagonia. (2011). *"Don't Buy This Jacket" Campaign.* Company Archive.

113. Patterson, Kerry, Grenny, Joseph, McMillan, Ron, and Switzler, Al. (2002). *Crucial Conversations: Tools for Talking When Stakes Are High.* McGraw-Hill.

114. Patterson, Kerry, Grenny, Joseph, McMillan, Ron, and Switzler, Al. (2002). *Crucial Conversations: Tools for Talking When Stakes Are High.* McGraw-Hill.

115. Pink, Daniel H. (2009). *Drive: The Surprising Truth About What Motivates Us.* Riverhead Books.

116. Pixar Animation Studios. (2020). Pixar Archives.

117. Porter, Michael E. (1980). *Competitive Strategy: Techniques for Analyzing Industries and Competitors.* Free Press.

118. Raiffa, Howard. (1982). *The Art and Science of Negotiation.* Harvard University Press.

119. Rasiel, Ethan. (1999). *The McKinsey Way: Using the Techniques of the World's Top Strategic Consultants to Help You and Your Business.* McGraw-Hill Education.

120. Ries, Eric. (2011). *The Lean Startup: How Today's Entrepreneurs Use Continuous Innovation to Create Radically Successful Businesses.* Crown Business.

121. Ritzer, George. (2011). *McDonaldization: The Reader.* Pine Forge Press.

122. Roberts, Andrew. (2019). *Leadership in War: Essential Lessons from Those Who Made History.* Viking.

123. Sandel, Michael J. (2009). *Justice: What's the Right Thing to Do?* Farrar, Straus and Giroux.

124. Saunders, Harold H. (1991). *The Other Walls: The Politics of the Arab-Israeli Peace Process.* Princeton University Press.

125. S chelling, Thomas C. (1960). *The Strategy of Conflict.* Harvard University Press.

126. Schoemaker, Paul J.H. (1995). *Scenario Planning: A Tool for Strategic Thinking.* Sloan Management Review.

127. Schultz, Howard. (2011). *Onward: How Starbucks Fought for Its Life Without Losing Its Soul.* Rodale Books.

128. Schwartz, Peter. (1991). *The Art of the Long View: Planning for the Future in an Uncertain World.* Currency Doubleday.

129. Seligman, Martin. (2011). *Flourish: A Visionary New Understanding of Happiness and Well-Being.* Atria Books.

130. Senge, Peter M. (1990). *The Fifth Discipline: The Art & Practice of the Learning Organization.* Doubleday.

131. Senge, Peter M. (1990). *The Fifth Discipline: The Art and Practice of the Learning Organization.* Doubleday/Currency.

132. Shapley, Lloyd S. (1953). *A Value for n-Person Games.* Contributions to the Theory of Games. Princeton University Press.

133. Sharma, Carol Sanford. (2014). *The Responsible Entrepreneur: Four Game-Changing Archetypes for Founders, Leaders, and Impact Investors.* Jossey-Bass.

134. Shell, G. Richard. (1999). *Bargaining for Advantage: Negotiation Strategies for Reasonable People.* Penguin Books.

135. Shiller, Robert J. (2015). *Irrational Exuberance.* Princeton University Press.

136. Silver, Nate. (2012). *The Signal and the Noise: Why So Many Predictions Fail — but Some Don't.* Penguin Books.

137. Simmons, Annette. (2006). *The Story Factor: Inspiration, Influence, and Persuasion through the Art of Storytelling.* Basic Books.

138. Sinek, Simon. (2009). *Start with Why: How Great Leaders Inspire Everyone to Take Action.* Penguin Books.

139. Sinek, Simon. (2019). *The Infinite Game.* Portfolio.

140. Spence, Michael. (1973). *Job Market Signaling.* The Quarterly Journal of Economics.

141. Spotify. (2022). *How to drive with Spotify and Waze*.

142. Stackelberg, Heinrich von. (1934). *Market Structure and Equilibrium.* Springer.

143. Stiglitz, Joseph E. (2010). *Freefall: America, Free Markets, and the Sinking of the World Economy.* W.W. Norton & Company.

144. Sun Tzu. (1910). *The Art of War.* Oxford University Press (translated editions).

145. Surowiecki, James. (2004). *The Wisdom of Crowds: Why the Many Are Smarter Than the Few.* Doubleday.

146. Surowiecki, James. (2004). *The Wisdom of Crowds: Why the Many Are Smarter Than the Few.* Anchor Books.

147. Susskind, Lawrence, and Cruikshank, Jeffrey. (1987). *Breaking the Impasse: Consensual Approaches to Resolving Public Disputes.* Basic Books.

148. S yed, Matthew. (2015). *Black Box Thinking: Why Most People Never Learn from Their Mistakes—But Some Do.* Penguin Books.

149. Taleb, Nassim Nicholas. (2001). *Fooled by Randomness: The Hidden Role of Chance in Life and in the Markets.* Random House.

150. Taleb, Nassim Nicholas. (2012). *Antifragile: Things That Gain from Disorder.* Random House.

151. Tetlock, Philip E., and Gardner, Dan. (2015). *Superforecasting: The Art and Science of Prediction.* Crown.

152. Thaler, Richard H. (2015). *Misbehaving: The Making of Behavioral Economics.* W.W. Norton & Company.

153. Thaler, Richard H., and Sunstein, Cass R. (2008). *Nudge: Improving Decisions About Health, Wealth, and Happiness.* Penguin Books.

154. Toyota Motor Corporation. (1990). *U.S. Market Entry Strategies.* Company Archive.

155. Toyota Motor Corporation. (1997). *Launch of the Prius.*

156. Tucker, Albert W. (1950). *A Two-Person Dilemma.* Stanford University Press.

157. Tversky, Amos, and Kahneman, Daniel. (1974). Judgment Under Uncertainty: Heuristics and Biases. Science.

158. UN Habitat Report on Curitiba's BRT System. (2013).

159. United Nations. (1993). *The Oslo Accords: Framework and Implementation.* UN Archives.

160. United States Department of Justice. (2017). *Antitrust Case Filings*.

161. Ury, William. (1991). Getting Past No: Negotiating with Difficult People. Bantam Books.

162. Von Neumann, John, and Morgenstern, Oskar. (1944). Theory of Games and Economic Behavior. Princeton University Press.

163. Voss, Chris. (2016). *Never Split the Difference: Negotiating as If Your Life Depended on It*. Harper Business.

164. Wieser, Friedrich von. (1914). Theory of Social Economy.

165. Winfrey, Oprah. (2010). *Behind the Scenes*. OWN.

Here's another book by Quinn Voss that you might like